NEW YORK CITY

FOURTEEN GREAT WALKS THROUGH THE STREETS OF MANHATTAN

CAROLYN HANSEN   CATHLEEN PECK

Art direction and design	Dennis Gallagher and John Sullivan Visual Strategies, San Francisco [visdesign.com]
Maps	Kit Gallagher
Photography	Carolyn Hansen additional stock photos
Copy Editor	Elissa Rabellino
Printer	Overseas Printing Inc.
Publisher	PowerHiking Ltd.

Printed in China

PowerHiking

FOREWORD

We measured our time and distances with a GPS device and diligently noted the names of shops and restaurants. While they may change somewhat, we hope that you find them as fascinating as we did. There will be slight variations as you do the hikes and in your destinations. Everyone walks at a different pace and will spend more or less time exploring points of interest. The museums and monuments are destinations where you can spend much more or much less time, depending on your own agenda. Any mistakes in the directions or the maps are ours, and we hope that you will forgive small inaccuracies.

We are continually grateful to our power partners, John and Rodney, for their support of our endeavors. Our design team, John Sullivan and Dennis Gallagher, continue to amaze us with their creativity and skill. We are grateful to Hal Belmont at Overseas Printing Ltd. for his insight and counseling.

Carolyn Hansen, Cathleen Peck

THINGS TO KNOW BEFORE YOU GO

YOUR STYLE IN NEW YORK CITY

New Yorkers are sharp dressers and style is key. Be comfortable but chic and you will be able to go from sightseeing to dinner. Black is always an "in" color in New York and travels well. Summers are warm but be prepared with layers, particularly in the fall and winter months. It can rain anytime of the year, so bring an umbrella and light waterproof jacket.

SECURITY

Like all urban centers, there are unfriendly neighborhoods. ***PowerHiking New York City*** does not lead you into these neighborhoods. However, good advice for any city is to always be aware of your surroundings and keep close guard on your valuables.

GETTING ABOUT THE CITY

The taxi system is the way to get about Manhattan. They are plentiful and easy to flag down. Some do now take credit cards but all should have a meter for the cost. Taxi drivers in New York City come from all over the world so do not be surprised if your driver is not fluent in English. The subway system is also efficient and economic. There are system maps available and maps on each train. You can purchase MetroCards in the stations, the best way to go.

RESTAURANTS AND FOOD

New York City is famous for excellent restaurants and good food. There are many choices ranging from fine dining to the favorite neighborhood lair. Try as many as you can.

SIGHTSEEING

The New York City Pass is available online. You can save on major tourist attractions as most are included, and frequently there are special lines for those with the Pass. It is worth the cost and even includes museums. Lines can be quite long so it is a good idea to purchase tickets online before you go.

WHAT IS POWERHIKING?

PowerHiking is choosing to walk with a big agenda. It takes sightseeing to a new level of energy and interest and allows you to see and to do as much as possible. It is walking with a purpose that excites not only your senses but also your spirit as you visit a neighborhood, a beautiful park, or an iconic building. Your days are full of exhilarating experiences and exercise.

In New York City ***PowerHiking*** takes on a whole new meaning. New York City is powerful, dynamic, exciting, exhilarating, vibrant, energetic, pulsating, multi-cultural. There is history, art, architecture, and world renowned restaurants. It is a city designed to be explored on foot and ***PowerHiking New York City*** will introduce you to it as you explore its many wonders. We see and experience it all from early in the morning until late in the evening. Whether it is an early start to avoid a long line at The Empire State Building, a leisurely afternoon river cruise, or an evening of theater and late supper, the city is there for the experience.

Although we spend very full days and evenings ***PowerHiking*** the richness that is New York City, the walks can be divided into less strenuous excursions, with more time devoted to the pleasures of wandering through museums, parks and historical monuments. You may choose to spend only a few hours exploring the city or follow the longer routes that take you through many famous sites. The city is truly a feast to enjoy as you prefer. You are in charge of your experience, and walking from one destination to the next is the key. Wear your ***PowerHiking*** shoes, take a bottle of water, a camera, this book and set out on your ***PowerHiking*** adventure in New York City.

CONTENTS

1

LOWER MANHATTAN BATTERY PARK

- Battery Park
- Castle Clinton National Monument
- Statue of Liberty
- Ellis Island
- Museum of Jewish Heritage
- Museum of the American Indian
- Wall Street
- New York Stock Exchange
- The Bull
- Trinity Church
- St. Paul's Chapel
- Ground Zero
- The Winter Garden
- Irish Hunger Memorial
- Hudson River Parkway
- TriBeCa

TIME All day | **DISTANCE** 4 miles

Walker St
Beach St
N Moore St
White St
Centre St
TRIBECA
Leonard St
Worth St
Berry St
Market St
Catherine St
Madison
Cherry St
N River Piers
West St
Greenwich St
Hudson St
Duane St
Washington Market Park
Chambers St
Park Row
Governor Nelson A Rockefeller Park
Warren St
River Terrace
W Broadway
Frankfort St
Murray St
N End Ave
Church St
Franklin D Roosevelt Dr
Brooklyn Bridge
Irish Hunger Memorial
Vesey St
St. Paul's Chapel
Ann St
Ground Zero
World Financial Center & Winter Garden
Broadway
North Cove
Liberty St
Nassau St
William St
Cedar
Pearl St
Front St
South St
Albany St
American Stock Exchange
Pine St
Water St
Wall Street
Trinity Church
Museum of Jewish Heritage
Battery Pl
National Museum of the American Indian
E River Dr
Robert F Wagner Jr Park
Battery Park
South St
Castle Clinton
Ellis Island & Liberty Island Ferry

The southern tip of Manhattan Island and ***Battery Park*** are steeped in cultural history and this ***PowerHike*** explores the historical significance of this impressive locale, important from the Revolutionary War to the disembarkation of the immigrants who helped to shape this country with their first steps on American soil, to the terrorist attack of September 11, 2001. Overlooking the harbor, ***Battery Park*** is the largest area of open space in New York City. Once an artillery battery charged with protecting the island, and the scene of the departure of British soldiers following the

American Revolution, it was a site of grand mansions and promenades. One mansion still remains from its glory days, the *James Watson House*, just to the north of the park. **Castle Clinton National Monument** is the major landmark of the park, built just before the War of 1812. It became part of **Battery Park** when the park was created by landfill in the early 19th century. Popular as a theatrical venue and

instrumental in New York City's development as a theater mecca, **Castle Clinton** became an immigration depot as mansions were abandoned for uptown and immigrants began to populate the neighborhood.

The Battery is full of life. Just about anything is available for purchase from the spirited vendors. Wander through the park to take in the many memorials erected

there. Among others is the *Battery Cannon*, dating from the Revolutionary War, the *Marine Flagstaff*, *the Coast Guard Memorial for WWII*, the *New York Korean War Veterans Memorial*, *The Immigrants*, and the impressive *East Coast Memorial* commemorating those Americans missing in the Atlantic Ocean during WWII. On the Eisenhower Mall is *The Sphere* and eternal flame memorializing the victims of the 9/11 attack. *The Sphere* was located in the center of The World Trade Center and will return there once rebuilding is completed.

Battery Park is the location to board ferry boats to the ***Statue of Liberty*** and ***Ellis Island***. The lines are long so go early or purchase tickets in advance online. Be prepared for extensive security screening. The ferry runs frequently and you can disembark at ***Liberty Island*** and then re-embark to ***Ellis Island***. The ferry trip is a pleasurable way to view the remarkable skyline of Lower Manhattan. The ferry boat trip to ***Liberty Island*** is truly awe-inspiring. Given to the United States by France, this national monument is a symbol

of democracy, freedom and liberty. Walk around the island taking in the spectacular views of Manhattan and then go to the top of the ***Statue***, a must destination for

true *powerhikers*. Inside the ***Statue*** are exhibits explaining its history, with historical artifacts, the Torch Exhibit, a promenade featuring spectacular views of the harbor, Fort Wood, and the elevator to the observation deck. Audio tours are available in many languages as are guided tours by Park Rangers.

There is a gift shop with enticing souvenirs and a food concession.

Re-board the ferry for ***Ellis Island***, part of the ***Statue of***

Liberty National Monument. Originally responsible for harbor defense along with ***Castle Clinton***, this gateway to the US became the first federal immigration center in the country, from 1892 – 1954, when ***Castle Clinton*** could no longer handle

the growing number of immigrants. For many, ***Ellis Island*** was the first land they touched when coming to America. Inspection of papers and health took place in the *Registry Room* or *Great Hall* and the exhibits on ***Ellis Island*** are enlightening and fascinating. The tour of the ***Ellis Island Immigration Museum*** is self-guided, with a brochure to guide you along. There are also Park Ranger guided tours. As you enter the lobby, notice the display of suitcases and trunks from immigrants. Attend the historical play or the documentary film sharing experiences of immigrants. Following this introduction, you may choose to select an audio tour as you explore the *Great Hall* and view the rooms used for medical and legal examinations. There are even pillars where names carved by immigrants are visible. Exhibits explain the history of the island, the

immigrant experience, photo albums and family experiences as well as the culture and customs immigrants brought with them. In another room large sculptures and

maps explain the flow of immigrants over the years and the countries from which they came. Upstairs are several exhibits of photographs and artifacts of specific immigrant families. Walk to the outside park and the memorial of names. The large wall meanders throughout the island park listing the

name of every immigrant who passed through the island. Inside, the National Park Service provides computer service and assistance to trace family members and genealogy. There is a gift shop with ornaments, posters and other historical items and a cafeteria.

Take the ferry boat back to ***Battery Park***, enjoying the astonishing views of Lower Manhattan. Upon disembarking, continue this ***PowerHike*** through ***Battery Park*** and notice the remarkable gardens. Continue past the ***Sphere*** to *Battery Place* and left through ***Robert F. Wagner Jr. Park*** to the ***Museum of Jewish Heritage***, a

memorial to the Holocaust. There are personal belongings, photographs and stories of those who experienced the devastation, as well as theatrical presentations, musicals, films and lectures detailing the cultures of the Jewish communities and their enormous destruction. It is open daily except Saturdays, Jewish holidays and Thanksgiving. Return through the park to *Battery Place* and left to *Broadway*. To the right is the ***Museum of the American Indian***, part of the Smithsonian Institution. The collections cover life, culture, history and art of the Native American. The book shop carries informative

books as well as native jewelry, blankets and gift items. Continue left on *Broadway* to ***Wall Street*** and the ***New York Stock Exchange*** and the *Bull*. Behind you,

on Broadway, is ***Trinity Church***, dating from 1696 and listed on the National Register of Historic Places.

From ***Trinity Church,*** walk up *Trinity Place* towards the site of the World Trade Center,

Ground Zero. At *Liberty Street* cross the bridge to view the cavernous hole left on 9/11 by the collapse of the World Trade Center buildings. While plans to rebuild and maintain a memorial on the site are scheduled, the massive destruction remains as rebuilding continues at a slower pace than anticipated. At *Church Street* and *Vesey Street*, opposite the east side of ***Ground Zero***, is ***St. Paul's Chapel***, the oldest surviving church in the city. Dating from 1766, it is a National Historic Landmark. George Washington attended services here during the period when

New York City was the nation's capital. There are several artifacts of note including the original pew used by George Washington. During the attack of 9/11 and the collapse of the Twin Towers, ***St. Paul's Chapel*** remained standing and was a place of refuge for police, firemen and recovery workers as well as a location of personal memorials. To the west of ***Ground Zero*** are the ***World Financial Center*** and the ***Winter Garden,*** linked by a pedestrian

bridge. The ***Winter Garden*** was badly damaged during 9/11 but has been restored and is a spectacularly beautiful building. There are performances year round in this

stunning venue and in the summer they take place on the outdoor plaza overlooking *North Cove*. There are several

restaurants to relax in and enjoy. Exit on *Vesey Street* and go left to *North End Avenue* and the ***Irish Hunger Memorial***. Dedicated to the many who lost their lives in the Great Irish Famine, it is uniquely constructed of Irish soil, stone and vegetation. There is even a replica of a 19th century Irish cottage.

Continue walking along the Hudson River waterfront uptown towards ***TriBeCa***.

As you ***PowerHike***, appreciate the astonishing views of the huge buildings of the financial district, and of New Jersey across the river. The name ***TriBeCa*** derives from the first letters of the words *triangle below Canal Street*. Now a chic

residential neighborhood with trendy restaurants, it was once the hub of the textile industry. Warehouses were converted into lofts as artists moved in. Probably ***TriBeCa's*** most renowned denizen is the actor, Robert DeNiro, co-founder of the *TriBeCa Film Festival*. At *Chambers Street* turn right through ***Washington Market*** and ***Duane Park*** to *Greenwich Street*. Turn left on Greenwich to the heart of the hip restaurant scene. You will see DeNiro's ***Tribeca Grill***, a most celebrated restaurant, featuring local market cuisine and housed in an historic warehouse and designed to reflect the energy and excitement of the neighborhood. The outside terrace is perfect to watch the local dynamics. Turn right at *N. Moore Street* and then right on *Hudson Street* to encounter more

famous eateries. You will see ***Nobu***, spectacular Japanese cuisine, ***Bouley***, and ***Bubby's Pie Company***. ***Bubby's*** is a popular family eatery and the display of pies will tempt the strongest will.

As you conclude this ***PowerHike,*** choose one of the many neighborhood eateries to relax and enjoy a fine New York meal as you reflect on all that you have experienced on this most amazing and historical ***PowerHike***.

2

THE EMPIRE STATE BUILDING

The Empire State Building

The Morgan Library and Museum

Murray Hill

TIME **4** hours | **DISTANCE** **1** mile

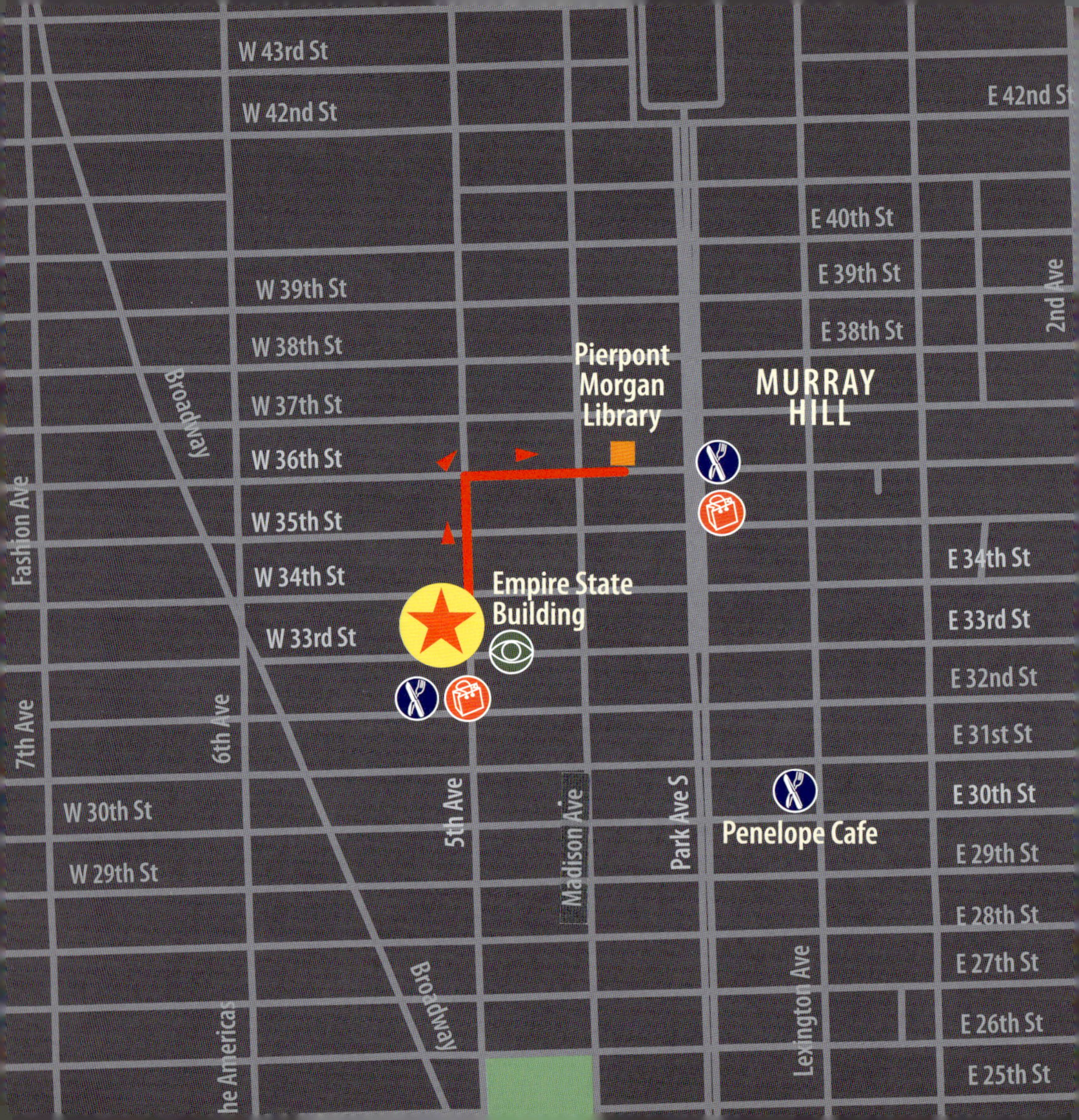

W 43rd St
W 42nd St
E 42nd St
E 40th St
E 39th St
E 38th St
2nd Ave
W 39th St
W 38th St
W 37th St
W 36th St
W 35th St
W 34th St
W 33rd St
Broadway
Pierpont
Morgan
Library
MURRAY
HILL
Fashion Ave
E 34th St
Empire State
Building
E 33rd St
E 32nd St
E 31st St
7th Ave
6th Ave
E 30th St
W 30th St
5th Ave
Madison Ave
Park Ave S
Penelope Cafe
E 29th St
W 29th St
E 28th St
E 27th St
Broadway
Lexington Ave
E 26th St
he Americas
E 25th St

Rising 1252 feet into the New York sky, ***The Empire State Building*** is synonymous with New York City. This iconic landmark dominates the skyline. Reaching 102 stories tall it can be seen for miles around. Above its art deco tower and dome rises an art deco spire and the entire tower area is awash at night with floodlights of ever changing colors. It was miraculously built in a little over one year and completed in 1931. Constructed under dangerous and precarious conditions and without modern day equipment, workers considered themselves lucky to be able to work on

this amazing edifice. It remains today not only an incredible building achievement, but also an architectural and structural marvel. ***PowerHike*** to *34th Street* and *Fifth Avenue*, the site of this art deco building, once the tallest skyscraper in the world. The lobby of the building is a glorious three-story entry. The ceiling is covered with recently renovated gold murals of the sky surrounded by marble panels. There is an enormous aluminum relief of ***The Empire State Building*** itself on the far wall and the bank of elevators has equally

impressive reliefs above each one. The lines to get in may be long so it is wise to go early and be prepared for extensive security screening. If you purchase a City Pass online (good for other venues as well), there are special accelerated lines. Visit the second floor *NY Skyride*, a simulated tour with an IMAX screen and motion seats. After that experience, follow the lines to the observatories. The wait in line is worth it because the views from the 86th floor observation deck are awe-inspiring. There are informative maps and audiphones to describe the vistas. Take time to familiarize yourself with the city below

and savor the panoramic views. There is also a smaller observatory on the 102nd floor, which is available for an additional admission ticket. Do

you remember the movies this famous skyscraper has been part of: *King Kong*, *An Affair To Remember*, *Sleepless In Seattle*? The spire above the 102nd floor was originally built for dirigible landings but proved ineffective, as the winds were too strong, and it is now a radio antenna. Spectacular as the views are in the daytime, at night the lights of New York City stretch before you as in a fairyland. The tower of the building itself is illuminated with floodlights of varying colors and can be seen throughout the city. Since its completion, the top of

the building has been illuminated but the lighting has become more significant and sophisticated throughout the years. There is a Tower Lights schedule and the lighting changes quite frequently commemorating special occasions, holidays and seasons. Visit the official building web site, www.esbnyc.com, to check the schedule. The observatory is open from 8AM to 2AM daily so you can visit more than once. You will want to visit the gift shop for a unique souvenir of

this exciting adventure or a snack.

Just up *Fifth Avenue* at *36th Street* and at the edge of *Murray Hill* is ***The Morgan Library and Museum***. Once the home of the financier, Pierpont Morgan, the library was donated to the city by his son, J.P. Morgan, Jr., honoring his father's dream that the collection belong to the public. Morgan was an avid collector of fine art and this unique museum has a fascinating collection of artistic, literary, and musical manuscripts. The majestic library in the Italian Renaissance style was built to house his magnificent collection, which is continually expanding. A must visit is the mogul's richly furnished study, an inspiring trip back in time. There is a café located in a glass-enclosed court, available

Wednesday through Sunday to museum ticket holders. *The Morgan Dining Room* is available for private events and is also available for lunch Tuesday through Sunday.

It is a wonderful experience dining in the original family dining room. *The Morgan Shop* is definitely worth a visit. More than a bookstore, there are many unique items to tantalize the shopper. The library is open Tuesday through Sundays and there is a charge for admission. However, the *Morgan Shop* and the *Morgan Dining Room* do not require a fee. Tours are available so check the web site, www.themorgan.org for times and current exhibits. If you wish to explore the ***Murray Hill*** neighborhood a bit, ***PowerHike***

towards *Lexington Avenue* and **Penelope Café** located at *30th Street* for a delightful New York experience and opportunity to reflect on this ***PowerHike.***

3

CENTRAL PARK WEST

- Columbus Circle
- Heckscher Playground and Ballfields
- Children's Carousel
- Sheep Meadow
- Strawberry Fields
- The Lake
- Bethesda Terrace
- Bow Bridge
- The Ramble
- Belvedere Castle
- Turtle Pond
- Shakespeare Garden
- Swedish Cottage
- Delacorte Theater
- The Great Lawn
- The Pinetum
- Diana Ross Playground
- Jacqueline Kennedy Onassis Reservoir

TIME **4-5** hours | **DISTANCE** **5+** miles

Jacqueline Kennedy Onassis Reservoir
Museum Mile
Central Park East Dr
E 90th St
W 90th St
Ross Pinetum
Diana Ross Playground
Transverse Rd
85th St
W 86th St
W 85th St
CENTRAL PARK
E 85th St
E 84th St
Great Lawn
Delecorte Theater
East Dr
W 81st St
Swedish Cottage
Shakespeare Garden
Turtle Pond
Belvedere Castle
Transverse Rd
E 79th St
Riverside Dr
W End Ave
Amsterdam Ave
Columbus Ave
W 77th St
Madison Ave
Park Ave
Lexington Ave
3rd Ave
2nd Ave
Boat House
The Lake
Bethesda Fountain Terrace
E 72nd St
Strawberry Fields
W 72nd St
Henry Hudson Pky
Broadway
Terrace Dr
Sheep Meadow
Center Dr
The Mall
East Dr
W 67th St
W 66th St
W 65th St
65th St
E 66th St
E 65th St
West Dr
Heckscher Playground
5th Ave
Central Park Dr
The Pond
E 60th St
W 60th St
W 59th St
W 59th St
Columbus

The most remarkable attraction in Manhattan is its centerpiece, ***Central Park***. Offering magnificent landscapes, lush flowers, statuary, lakes, and beautiful old trees, ***Central Park*** is an oasis of green in busy New York City and used by residents and visitors year round as a place of refuge, beauty and fun. Beautiful in all seasons, no trip to New York City is complete without visiting ***Central Park***. Take time to row around a lake, listen to a talented musician, or partake in refreshment from one of the many picturesque street vendors throughout the park. Even take a short ride through

part of the park in one of the timeless horse carriages, and bring your camera!

To make the most of your exploration of ***Central Park***, we divide the park into two ***PowerHikes***. The west side ***PowerHike*** begins on *59th Street* or *Central Park* South. Enter on *6th Avenue, 7th Avenue* or ***Columbus Circle***, location of the famous *Maine Monument* and many street vendors and entertainers. This ***PowerHike*** enters at *6th Avenue*, through what is known as the ***Artists' Gate***. In the plaza are

imposing statues of José de San Martin, Simon Bolivar, and José Julian Martí. *Sixth Avenue* at *Central Park South* is known as *Avenue of the Americas*, and these bronze equestrian statues acknowledge the leaders of Latin American independence. Follow the paved roadway to the left until you reach *West Drive*. Turn right on *West Drive* walking uptown. On your right you will pass ***Umpire Rock***, a huge outcropping of native rock, and ***Heckscher Playground and Ballfields***. This is a very busy part of ***Central Park*** as you will see ball games and families having fun at all times. On the far side of the ball fields is the ***Children's***

Carousel. Cross *65th Street Traverse Drive* onto the path to ***Sheep Meadow***. There were sheep on this huge green until 1934. Today the 15 acre meadow is used for relaxing and enjoying magnificent views of the surrounding skyline. To the left is the Tavern on the Green. This famous Victorian-style building opened as a restaurant in 1934 complete with Tiffany glass and crystal chandeliers. The surrounding trees are covered in little fairy lights.

As you continue on *West Drive*, ahead is the ***Lawn Bowling and Croquet Greens*** and across Olmsted and Vaux Way on the left is ***Strawberry Fields***, a small section of the park dedicated as a garden of peace and the location of some of ***Central***

Park*'s* most beautiful trees. ***Strawberry Fields*** is located just inside *Central Park West* at *72nd Street* where *Beatle*, John Lennon, lived in the famous Dakota.

The Imagine Mosaic, memorial to John Lennon, is in the center of the area where he loved to walk. Both ***Strawberry Fields*** and ***Imagine*** are named after Lennon's songs.

To the right on *West Drive* is ***The Lake***. Surrounded by magnificent trees and

views of high-rise buildings, it is adjacent to the beautiful ***Bethesda Terrace***. Walk down the steps to view the ***Bethesda Arcade*** and ***Bethesda Fountain***, *the* ***Angel of the Waters***. At the boathouse on the east side of ***The Lake*** you can rent rowboats to explore the water. Continue around the west side of ***The Lake*** to ***Bow Bridge***, an icon of the park. Across ***Bow Bridge*** is ***The Ramble***. A maze of paths, birdlife, and native vegetation, ***The Ramble*** is different

from the rest of the park, more dense and natural. It is worth exploring to find ***Azalea Pond***, the ***Cave*** and the ***Stone Arch***.

As you exit ***The Ramble*** on the north side of ***The Lake*** and cross the *79th Street Traverse*, you catch site of ***Belvedere Castle*** *and* ***Vista Rock***. It is considered the most striking architectural feature in

Central Park. Designed by Calvert Vaux in 1867, in a mixture of Norman, Gothic and Moorish styles, its three terraces look out over the park's most sparkling vistas. **Belvedere Castle** is a favorite spot for bird watchers and has weather instruments in the tower for predicting weather in the park. Just below **Belvedere Castle** is **Turtle Pond,** a lovely small lake that is a nature blind and named after the many turtle residents. You can see them sunning themselves on the rocks.

To the left or west of the castle is the ***Shakespeare Garden***. William Shakespeare loved flowers and the garden is full of roses and flowers mentioned in his works. The garden sits mostly on rock but is a visual treat. A group known as the Shakespeare Gardeners cares for it. Immediately to the left of the garden is the ***Swedish Cottage***, formerly known as the Swedish Schoolhouse. Originally part of the Philadelphia Centennial Exhibition, the schoolhouse has had various purposes over the years. It is now a marionette theater, delighting children of all ages with puppet

shows of magical fairy tales. Tickets and reservations are required and there is a private room available for birthday parties and other private events.

Just beyond the ***Swedish Cottage*** and ***Shakespeare Garden*** is the ***Delacorte Theater***, home of the New York Shakespeare Festival. A summer institution in the park, these performances are free and a summer in Manhattan is not complete without attending a performance at the beautiful outdoor ***Delacorte Theater***. Tickets are available the day of the performance.

To the right of the ***Delacorte Theater*** and just a few steps over the *86th Street Transverse Road* is ***The Great Lawn***. One of the park's most popular spots, it is located on what was once the Croton River Reservoir. During the

Depression era the reservoir became outdated and was drained. It was then filled with material excavated from Rockefeller Center and an immense grass lawn with playing fields was created. It has been the site of concerts by the New York Philharmonic, the Metropolitan Opera, Luciano Pavarotti, Elton John, Placido Domingo, Simon and Garfunkel and many more. ***The Great Lawn*** is used by many for playing, sunbathing and quiet time as well, and the Central Park Conservancy controls the use to protect the beauty of the location.

Continue to ***PowerHike*** northward along ***The Great Lawn*** path to the ***Ross Pinetum***, passing the ***Diana Ross Playground*** and ***Summit Rock*** on the left. Park benefactor, Arthur Ross, planted ***The Pinetum*** in 1971. There are hundreds of species of pines from around the world, but the majority are White Pine and Himalayan Pine. This is a great spot for a picnic or just to relax, as the trees are magnificent and there are many benches with spectacular vistas.

Just beyond ***The Pinetum*** is the ***Jacqueline Kennedy Onassis Reservoir***. Before reaching the reservoir, you cross the *85th Street Transverse* and a bridle path that circles the reservoir, and encounter one of three magnificent Victorian bridges. The other two are located around the reservoir. Once part of the city's water system, now joggers and walkers mostly use the trail next to the reservoir. ***PowerHike*** around the Reservoir, if you choose, a distance of 1.6 miles, and take in the superb views of the surrounding high rise buildings. The reservoir's northern end is at *96th Street* but ***Central Park*** continues as far north as *110th Street* or *Central Park North*. Beyond the reservoir is the ***North Meadow***, ***The Ravine***, with its boulders and cascades, and the ***Harlem Meer***, a lake known for its catch and release fishing.

To return to *Central Park South* and your New York power evening, ***PowerHike*** back through the many fascinating venues that you have just visited, or you can head south on *East Drive* and see a bit of what awaits you in the ***PowerHike*** of ***Central Park East***. At the *72nd Street Transverse* go right and you are at the beautiful

Bethesda Terrace again. Cross the street and stroll back along ***The Mall***, a splendid walkway under majestic elm trees. It is a fitting ending to a superb ***PowerHike***. ***The Mall*** will lead you to *Central Park Drive* and a return to the ***Artists' Gate***. Across the street a good New York meal awaits you at *Mickey Mantle's* or *Sara Beth's*, or head down *Central Park South* to one of the fine restaurants in the *Time Warner Center*.

4

CENTRAL PARK EAST

- Grand Army Plaza
- The Pond
- Hallett Nature Preserve
- Wollman Rink
- Heckscher Ballfields
- The Carousel
- The Dairy
- The Zoo
- The Mall
- Bethesda Fountain
- The Lake
- The Conservatory Water
- Hans Christian Anderson Statue
- Alice in Wonderland Statue
- Still Hunt Statue
- Central Park Obelisk
- Jacqueline Kennedy Onassis Reservoir
- Conservancy Garden and Vanderbilt Gate
- Museum Mile

TIME 5 hours | **DISTANCE** 6 miles

Conservatory Garden
The Pool
North Meadow
East Dr
East Meadow
5th Ave
96th Transverse Rd
Museum Mile
Jacqueline Kennedy Onassis Reservoir
85th Transverse Rd
CENTRAL PARK
Turtle Pond
79th Transverse Rd
Alice in Wonderland
Hans Christian Anderson
Conservatory Water
The Lake
Terrace Dr
Bethesda Terrace
Center Dr
The Mall
65th St
West Dr
Wollman Memorial Rink
Central Park
The Pond
W 59th St
Grand Army Plaza
Riverside Dr
W 100th St
W End Ave
W 97th St
W 96th St
W 90th St
W 86th St
W 85th St
W 81st St
W 77th St
Amsterdam Ave
Columbus Ave
Central Park W
W 72nd St
Broadway
W 67th St
W 66th St
W 65th St
W 60th St
7th Ave
W 56th St
E 102nd St
E 97th St
E 96th St
E 90th St
E 85th St
E 84th St
E 79th St
E 72nd St
Madison Ave
Park Ave
Lexington Ave
3rd Ave
2nd Ave
1st Ave
York Ave
E 66th St
E 65th St
E 60th St
E 59th St
E 55th St
FDR Dr

Central Park is the vibrant green oasis that is the heart and soul of Manhattan.

Filled with New Yorkers, tourists, and colorful vendors, it is a "must do" when visiting New York City. The park changes with the seasons and activities change as well – tennis, ice skating, boating, baseball, soccer, jogging, and bicycling – it is full of activities to enjoy at any time of

the year. Whether the ground is covered with snow or the daffodils are just bursting forth framing spectacularly colorful azaleas, the park is breathtaking in every season. In 1857 Frederick Law Olmsted and Calvert Vaux presented a plan to the city Central Park Commission

to create a traditional English landscape in an area of rocks and swamp. It was an incredibly immense undertaking with carts and horses used to remove the mud and bring in topsoil. The park first opened a short two years later in 1859 and was declared a National Historic Landmark in 1964. New Yorkers first enjoyed winter ice skating, followed by carriage parades, summer concerts, and bicycling. Tennis courts and the ***Carousel*** came next. In 1871 the ***Zoo*** was added along with playgrounds and athletic fields. Of course,

Central Park has changed over the years. Where there were once carriage rides, there are now marches and races. It has been used in TV and movies and there is even a location for weddings at the ***Conservatory Garden***. Restoration of many of the original buildings and lawn areas has been the responsibility of the Central Park Conservancy, a private organization using both public and private funds. It took over in 1980 and is currently responsible for maintenance of the park. The Conservancy has kiosks throughout the park with maps, brochures, and information.

The ***Central Park East PowerHike*** starts at ***Grand Army Plaza*** and ***Pulitzer Fountain*** at the corner of *Central Park South (59th Street*) and *Fifth Avenue*. On the south side of the plaza is the ***Pulitzer Fountain***, built with money donated by Joseph Pulitzer, and on the north side of the plaza is the ***Sherman Monument***. It is the park's grandest monument and spectacularly marks the main entrance to ***Central Park***. Walk up *East Drive* and ***The Pond*** is on the left. With its beautifully curved

shape of water surrounded by a glorious variety of trees, you feel removed from the city while being only a few steps inside the park. Bordering ***The Pond*** is the ***Hallett Nature Sanctuary***, where a large array of migratory birds can be seen, but by Conservancy tours only. Just beyond ***The Pond*** is the ***Wollman Rink***. Open to the public from October to April for ice skating, the venue is a favorite of New Yorkers and has been seen in many movies. During the summer months ***Wollman Rink*** becomes an amusement park. Further up on the left and beyond the ***Heckscher Ballfields*** is the ***Carousel***, a favorite park attraction. To the right of the ***Carousel*** is the historic old ***Dairy***. Originally built in a Victorian Gothic style, this uniquely beautiful building is the official park information center and gift shop. On the right side of *East Drive* is another park favorite, the ***Zoo***. It is the nation's first zoo and the humorous statue, ***Amusing Bear***, is a treat. The entrance to the ***Zoo*** is the ***Delacorte Clock***. Whimsical animals such as a bear, a goat, a penguin, and a kangaroo play nursery rhymes throughout the day and seasonal music during the holidays. Just beyond the

Zoo on the left is ***The Mall***. While you will miss the ***East Green*** and many of the park's flowering trees, veer left to ***The Mall***. Lined by magnificent elm trees and sculptures of literary and poetic giants, this is a walk to be savored. At the northern end of ***The Mall*** is the ***Concert Ground***, a beautiful Beaux Arts shell. Across the street are ***Bethesda Terrace***, ***Bethesda Arcade***, and ***Bethesda Fountain*** overlooking ***The Lake***. We explore this area in the ***Central Park West*** chapter, but it is such a splendid setting that it is worth seeing again. Return to *East Drive* and be sure not to miss ***Balto*** on your return hike. ***Balto*** stands guard just north of the ***Zoo*** and just south of the ***East Green***. He is an

Alaskan Husky and a favorite of children visiting the park.

Continue north on *East Drive* to one of the most whimsical parts of the park. Pass ***Pilgrim Hill***, with the beautiful flowering cherry trees, to the ***Conservatory***

Water. This small pond is a destination for many who visit the park regularly and is always surrounded with children and adults sailing model boats. If you wish to join the fun, boats can be rented at ***the Kerbs Boat House*** on the west side of ***The Pond***. Enjoy and have fun! There is a café there as well. On the east side of

the ***Conservatory Water*** is a statue enjoyed by all ages, ***Hans Christian Anderson***. This is a favorite gathering spot of the park's group of bird watchers. Just a few steps beyond is another popular statue in the park, ***Alice In Wonderland***, sitting atop a giant mushroom and surrounded by the Mad Hatter and the March Hare.

Continue ***PowerHiking*** up *East Drive* and near *76th Street* look up to the left and there is ***Still Hunt***, a life size bronze

panther crouching on a huge rock overlooking the path, lifelike and ready to pounce. A little further on the right is the back of the *Metropolitan Museum of Art*. One of the world's most famous museums, we visit it in another chapter. To the left is the ***Central Park Obelisk***, surrounded by beautiful flowering cherry and magnolia trees. Just beyond is the ***Jacqueline Kennedy Onassis Reservoir***. This is a destination for

walkers and joggers and offers some of the best views of the high rise buildings surrounding the park. Join the many walkers, counter clockwise only, and ***PowerHike*** the 1.6 mile path.

East Drive continues past the ***East Meadow*** with its array of magnificent old trees to the ***Conservatory Garden***. Located at the northern part of the park at *105th Street* and *Fifth Avenue*, entry is through the famous ***Vanderbilt Gate***, which used to stand at the Vanderbilt mansion. Comprised of three different gardens, the ***Conservatory***

Garden is an oasis of serenity and beauty just steps from the busy streets of Manhattan. Take time to wander through and enjoy this classical setting: the *North Garden*, a French garden with fountains and huge seasonal flower beds, the *Central Garden*, an Italian style garden that is a favorite site of

weddings, and the *South Garden*, more of an English garden with a reflecting pool, pathways, hedges and abundant perennials. The gardens are open daily. Check times for the free tours. At the northernmost part of ***Central Park*** is ***Harlem Meer***, another one of the park's bodies of water, surrounded by great old trees and site of many activities for children and families.

To conclude this ***PowerHike*** we exit the park and stroll down the cobbled sidewalks

of *Fifth Avenue* towards *Central Park South*. Marvel at the trees of the park and the magnificent residences overlooking the park. Enjoy the street vendors and take note of the several museums which we visit in another chapter. At *59th Street* turn right to the many restaurants waiting for you. After a long ***PowerHike*** you deserve a delicious New York meal and time to reflect on the beauty and wonders of ***Central Park***.

5

FIFTH AVENUE

- Plaza Hotel
- Garden Court
- Shops at the Plaza
- Oak Bar
- Pulitzer Fountain
- Fifth Avenue
- Trump Tower
- St. Patrick's Cathedral
- Rockefeller Center
- Radio City Music Hall
- Magnolia Bakery
- St. Thomas Church
- Museum of Modern Art
- Peninsula Hotel

TIME All Day | **DISTANCE** **8** miles

HALL BE THE
GE BUILDIN
GE BUI DING
ER IN EVERY ART BROUGHT THE
TO MORTA S A MEANS TO MIGHTY

CENTRAL PARK
Central Park
W 59th St
The Plaza Hotel
5th Ave
E 61st St
E 60th St
E 59th St
Pulitzer Fountain
W 58th St
E 58th St
Bergdorf Goodman
W 57th St
E 57th St
Avenue of the Americas
Trump Tower
E 56th St
7th Ave
W 56th St
W 55th St
Four Seasons Hotel
W 54th St
Museum of Modern Art
W 53rd St
Broadway
St. Thomas Church
W 52nd St
Swing St
W 51st St
Radio City Music Hall
St. Patrick's Cathedral
Magnolia Bakery
W 50th St
Rainbow Room
Saks Fifth Avenue
W 49th St
Rockafeller Center
E 48
W 48th St
E 47
W 47th St
5th Ave
Madison Ave
E 46
E 45

The Plaza Hotel, located at *Fifth Avenue* and *Central Park South,* is the starting point for the **Fifth Avenue PowerHike**. This grand dame is a New York City treasure and the setting for countless movies such as *Crocodile Dundee, The Way We Were, Home Alone* and TV shows *The Sopranos* and *Sex in the City*. Recently remodeled with elegant residences on the upper floors and a luxury boutique hotel below, **The Plaza** remains an exquisite example of *Beaux Arts* grandeur and luxury. Walk past the impeccably garbed doorman, through the illustrious doors and into

the impressive lobby, steeped in luxury and tradition. Beyond the magnificent chandelier is the *Garden Court*, where tea is served September through May. As you take in the historical splendor, venture down the escalator to the new *Shops at*

the Plaza. An art gallery, jewelry, clothing, flowers, chocolates, European beauty products, spa, salon, fitness center, and sweet shops will all tempt you. Not to be missed in the evening is the renowned *Oak Bar*. It is one of New York's most famous bars and a place to see and be seen. Upon leaving the ***Plaza Hotel***, to the left is ***Central Park*** (which we explore in another **PowerHike**) and the statue of *General Sherman*. Across the street beyond the Plaza Hotel Rolls Royce, is the *Pulitzer Fountain, Abundance*. Cross and you are now on glamorous ***Fifth Avenue***, lined on both sides with famous stores and

European designer boutiques. This is unquestionably one of the most famous streets in the world. While ***Fifth Avenue*** is best known for shopping, it is also a major artery of the city and the location of many parades throughout the year. Maybe you will be lucky enough to see an Irish, Polish, or Hare Krishna parade, or the very famous Easter Parade.

Join the crowds and enjoy!

On your right at *58th Street* is *Bergdorf Goodman*.One of New York's most famous retailers, the store is located on the site of the mansion of Cornelius Vanderbilt II. The art deco building is a fashion mecca, and has a lovely restaurant with beautiful city and park views. Exit on **Fifth Avenue** and cross at *57th Street*, walking east towards *Madison Avenue*, passing famous European designers such as *Louis Vuitton, Burberry*, and *Chanel*. At *Madison Avenue* cross and return back up 57th Street, passing the flagship *NIKE Store*. At **Fifth Avenue** turn left and window shop the many designer boutiques as you make your way towards *50th Street* and **Rockefeller Center**. Enjoy gazing at *Cartier*, *Henri*

Bendel, Gucci, Escada, Bulgari, Prada, Versace, Ferragamo, Brooks Brothers, the *Disney Store*, and just about every other big name that you can imagine. If you are tempted, step inside for a closer look. Across ***Fifth Avenue*** is the *NBA Store* where visitors can entertain themselves shooting baskets. Between *57th Street* and *56th Street* is ***The Trump Tower***. The atrium in this spectacular glass and marble building is

world famous, and riding the escalator to the top is a visual treat. The elegant *Trump Grill* is located on the first floor of the *Atrium Tower*, a special setting for a beverage or a meal. On the lower level is a café next to the amazing *Atrium Tower* waterfall.

Continue on ***Fifth Avenue*** taking time to browse the colorful New York street vendors. From hot dogs to scarves, pretzels to handbags, grilled nuts to fruit and ethnic dishes, it is all enticing. Located between *51st Street* and *50th Street* is ***St. Patrick's Cathedral.*** Declared a National Historic

Landmark, this Neo-Gothic cathedral has quite a history and luminous stained glass windows. It is definitely worthwhile to see before continuing the **PowerHike**. Just across *50th Street* and with its array of American flags fluttering in the breeze,

is *Saks Fifth Avenue*. For a truly New York shopping experience, visit this high-voltage department store, a fixture in the city since 1924. If you visit during the holidays, the windows are most attractively decorated and

surrounded by crowds trying to get a glimpse.

After experiencing *Saks*, cross ***Fifth Avenue*** to ***Rockefeller Center***. Framed by beautiful fountains and attractive flower beds imaginatively planted year round, the unique art deco buildings are a National Historic Landmark and home to *NBC Studios*. If you can tear yourself away from the wonderful boutiques, florists and chocolate shops, walk towards the flags. The famous fountain with the bronze statue of *Prometheus*

is in front of you. During spring and summer, *Rock Center Café, The Sea Grill*, and *The Rink Bar* have tables outside by the fountain for a relaxing break. In the late fall and winter, the area is transformed into an ice skating rink, one of the city's most

popular attractions. Above the fountain is the site of the famous Christmas tree lighting ceremony, and both tourists and New Yorkers share in the merriment. ***PowerHike*** through ***Rockefeller Center*** westward in the direction of *6th Avenue*, allowing time to visit the observation deck of this beautiful art deco building. Studio tours are available and the ***Rainbow Room*** at the top is a special locale for incredible views. On the corner of *6th Avenue* and *49th Street* is ***Radio City Music Hall***. The theater is an architectural gem, and the famous marquee proclaims that the ***Music Hall*** is

home to the dancing performances of the *Rockettes*, the NFL draft, music concerts, and other events. It is most famous for the Christmas spectacular, the Nutcracker.

Next to ***Radio City Music Hall***, at 1240 Avenue

of the Americas (6th Avenue) is ***Magnolia Bakery***. The line will be out the door for this well-known bakery, but it is worth the wait for one of their super delicious cupcakes or souvenir tee shirts.

Return back to ***Fifth Avenue*****,** and turn left walking up to *53rd Street* and *St. Thomas Church*, famous for its boys' choir. Peek inside and you might hear a rehearsal. A left turn leads to the main entrance of ***MOMA***, because a visit to New York is not complete without a visit to the ***Museum of Modern Art***. The building was recently

remodeled and is worthy of a tour on its own, not to mention the extraordinary collection. The museum store has wonderful books and gift items and there are welcoming cafes and a lovely restaurant. After your enjoyable visit to ***MOMA***, return to ***Fifth Avenue*** and continue to *54th Street* and the *Peninsula Hotel*. Visit the roof bar which affords an exceptional view up and down ***Fifth Avenue***. It is a perfect setting to reflect on the many and varied sights of this **PowerHike**. As New York is "the city that never sleeps," enjoy the lights of ***Rockefeller Center*** and ***Fifth Avenue*** in the evening, perhaps followed by dinner at *China Grill* on *53rd Street*, or one of the many other fine midtown dining experiences.

6

UPPER EAST SIDE

Grand Army Plaza

Fifth Avenue

Metropolitan Museum of Art

Jewish Museum

Museum of the City of New York

Cooper Hewitt National Design Museum

Solomon R. Guggenheim Museum

Whitney Museum of American Art

Frick Collection

Madison Avenue

TIME All day | **DISTANCE** **3** miles

not accounting for inside the museums

Museum of the City of New York
Jewish Museum
Cooper-Hewitt National Design Museum
Guggenheim Museum
Metropolitan Museum of Art
Whitney Museum of American Art
Frick Collection
Serendipity
Bloomingdale's
Grand Army Plaza
UPPER EAST SIDE
Central Park
Harlem Meer
The Pool
Jacqueline Kennedy Onassis Reservoir
Turtle Pond
The Lake
The Pond
Transverse Rd
Terrace Dr
Center Dr
East Dr
West Dr
Park Dr S
Central Park East
Central Park W
Central Park N
Museum Mile
5th Ave
Madison Ave
Park Ave
Lexington Ave
3rd Ave
2nd Ave
1st Ave
York Ave
East End Ave
FDR Dr
Riverside Dr
W End Ave
Amsterdam Ave
Columbus Ave
Broadway
Joe DiMaggio Hwy
7th Ave
West Rd
Main St
W 109th St
W 108th St
W 107th St
W 106th St
W 100th St
W 97th St
W 96th St
W 90th St
W 86th St
W 85th St
W 81st St
W 77th St
W 72nd St
W 67th St
W 66th St
W 65th St
W 60th St
W 59th St
W 56th St
65th St
E 108th St
E 109th St
E 102nd St
E 97th St
E 96th St
E 90th St
E 85th St
E 84th St
E 79th St
E 75th St
E 74th St
E 72nd St
E 70th St
E 66th St
E 65th St
E 60th St
E 59th St

This ***PowerHike*** ventures into one of New York City's most desirable neighborhoods, the ***Upper East Side***. Elegant residential buildings grace *Fifth Avenue* and overlook *Central Park*, and uniformed doormen watch over stately buildings along *Park Avenue*. Many famous and well-known New Yorkers call this part of Manhattan home. Mansions and brownstones were built as wealthy New Yorkers abandoned the southern part of the island for midtown. Our ***PowerHike*** explores this neighborhood and what is called *Museum Mile*. While we visit and describe all of the museums, it is too much for one day. Plan your schedule to suit your own interests and choose the museums you wish to visit. The ***PowerHike*** can be separated into smaller

cultural adventures, and your visits need not be rushed.

Start at *Grand Army Plaza* on the corner of *Fifth Avenue* and *Central Park South*. While you can **PowerHike** through *Central Park* to our destinations, we walk it in another chapter so instead walk to the ***Upper East Side*** over the cobblestone sidewalks on *Fifth Avenue* along the outer edge of *Central Park*. Take time to enjoy the colorful street vendors while admiring the luxurious buildings across the avenue. At *82nd Street* you arrive at the ***Metropolitan Museum of Art***. A

visit to New York City is not complete without seeing the ***Met.*** Worth an entire day's visit and more, you will be in awe of this museum, founded in 1870. It has grown

into one of the largest and finest museums in the world, housing many familiar and famous master pieces. There are docent tours, audio tours, and maps to guide you around the enormous space. During your stay, you can relax in the *Petrie Court*

Café and *Wine Bar*, the *New American Wing Café*, the cafeteria, or, on weekends, the *Great Hall Balcony Bar*. Members may also use the *Trustees' Dining Room*. The extensive Museum Store is a tempting place for gifts and it has an exemplary selection of books. Conclude your visit to the **Met** on the roof to view the current sculpture exhibit and the *Roof Garden Café* and *Martini Bar*. You will be entranced by the experience as well as the dramatic views of the skyline and over *Central Park*.

After a long day at the ***Met***, it is time to relax, reflect, and enjoy the city and, perhaps, a Broadway show or good New York meal. *Note: The Met is closed on Mondays.*

Our ***PowerHike*****,** however, continues on to what you could plan for another day. Turn left out of the ***Met*** and continue uptown on *Fifth Avenue* to *92nd Street* and the ***Jewish Museum***. Housed in the beautifully restored Warburg mansion, the exhibits of Jewish history, painting, and culture are remarkable and unparalleled, as is the permanent exhibit, *Culture and Continuity: The Jewish Journey*. There is *Café Weissman* on the lower level, offering delicious fare along with kosher cuisine, and a small gift

shop. The museum is closed on Wednesdays.

Further uptown across *Fifth Avenue* from the *Conservatory Garden* at *102nd Street* is the **Museum of the City of New York**. It is a fascinating museum dedicated to exploring the history, diversity, culture and change over the years of the city. It offers not only exhibits but also

lectures and programs on every aspect of the city. You will want to see the museum shop, filled with New York City memorabilia. (Closed on Mondays.)

Return downtown on *Fifth Avenue* to *91st Street* and the **Cooper Hewitt National Design Museum**. It is located in what was once the *Andrew Carnegie Mansion* in the area of the city between *91st Street* and *96th Street* known as *Carnegie Hill*. It is part of the Smithsonian Institution and is dedicated to the exploration, understanding, and impact of design. Open daily, there is the lovely Arthur Ross Terrace and Garden, available May through September, which the Café overlooks. The shop features uniquely designed gifts and books.

Continue walking downtown on *Fifth Avenue* to the ***Solomon R. Guggenheim Museum***, the spectacular facade coming into view as you approach *89th Street*. An architectural icon of the city, the ***Guggenheim*** is a remarkable venue dedicated to contemporary

art of the 20th and 21st centuries and is part of a world wide network of museums. It was built in 1959 and designed by famous architect Frank Lloyd Wright. It is a significant architectural landmark and the great rotunda is fascinating. Visiting this unique building is an unforgettable experience as you browse the exhibits strolling up the circular rotunda walkway. There is a gift shop with unusual and modern gifts, clothing and toys and a noteworthy book selection. (Closed on Thursdays.)

Continue walking downtown on ***Fifth Avenue***. At *75th Street* turn left to *Madison*

Avenue and the **Whitney Museum of American Art**. Closed on Monday and Tuesday, there are free daily tours of galleries and exhibitions. There is a café on the lower level and the store has a wonderful selection of books and gifts reflecting 20th and 21st century American art. Founded in 1930 by Gertrude Vanderbilt Whitney to exhibit the work of living American artists, the museum first opened in Greenwich Village. The current location opened in 1966. The permanent collection began with the collection of Mrs. Whitney and has grown through donations over the years. Both the permanent collection and the temporary exhibits are rich in known and unknown contemporary artists.

Return to *Fifth Avenue* and *71st Street* and the **Frick Collection**. Beautifully

housed in the former mansion of Henry Clay Frick, not only is the collection impressive but the furnishings and gardens are also

stunning. It is the location of the Frick Art Reference Library.

At his death in 1919,

Henry Clay Frick bequeathed his mansion and most of his art and sculpture for a public gallery. His

purpose was to encourage interest in the fine arts. This is a very picturesque and captivating museum to visit. (Closed on Mondays.) Turn left when leaving the ***Frick*** and return to

Madison Avenue. A right turn leads you to a famous New York City shopping destination with couture boutiques lining both sides of ***Madison Avenue*** all the way to *57th Street*. Window shopping is entertaining, but to enter the locked and guarded shops one needs an appointment. There are several delightful cafés as you stroll along, perfect for relaxation and refreshment. There is also *Fred's* at *Barneys New York* at *East 61st Street.* Following such a jam-packed day, it is time to enjoy the evening in the city that never sleeps. Choose a favorite restaurant from one of the other chapters or venture to ***Time Warner Center*** or ***Times Square*** to one of the many delicious New York eateries. If energy permits, stroll east on *59th Street* passing *Bloomingdales*, to *Serendipity*. Famous as the location for the movie of the

same name, the restaurant is hugely popular and reservations are a must. Whatever your choice, relax and reflect on the many treasures of New York City.

7 POWERFUL CROSSTOWN BUILDINGS

United Nations Headquarters

Ralph Bunche Plaza

Tudor City

Ford Foundation Building

Chrysler Building

Grand Central Station

New York Public Library

Bryant Park

TIME **7** hours | **DISTANCE** **8** miles

depending on time spent at the UN, Grand Central, the Library

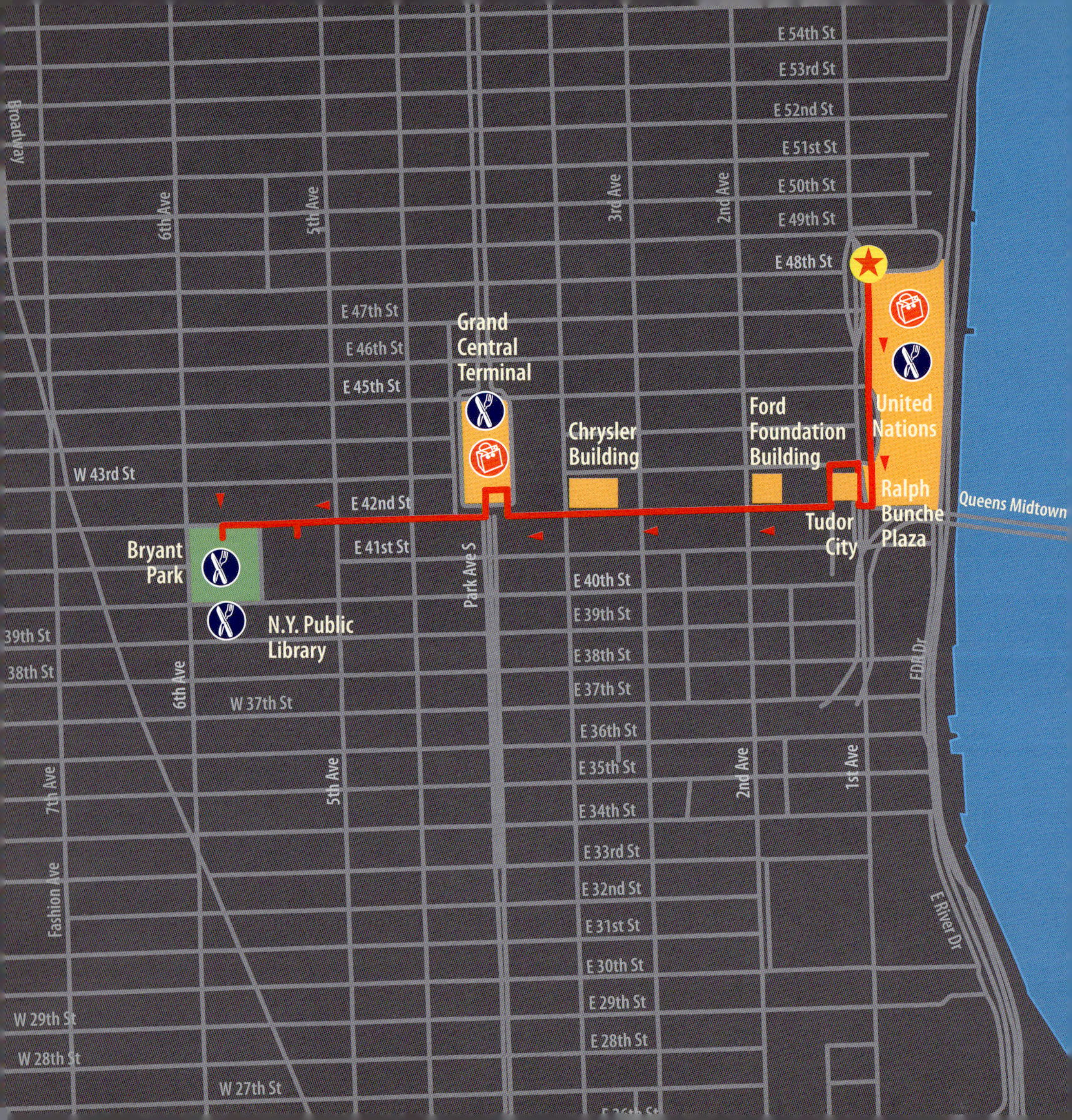
E 54th St
E 53rd St
E 52nd St
E 51st St
E 50th St
E 49th St
E 48th St
E 47th St
E 46th St
E 45th St
W 43rd St
E 42nd St
E 41st St
E 40th St
E 39th St
39th St
E 38th St
38th St
E 37th St
W 37th St
E 36th St
E 35th St
E 34th St
E 33rd St
E 32nd St
E 31st St
E 30th St
E 29th St
W 29th St
E 28th St
W 28th St
W 27th St
Broadway
6th Ave
5th Ave
3rd Ave
2nd Ave
1st Ave
7th Ave
Fashion Ave
Park Ave S
FDR Dr
E River Dr
Queens Midtown
Grand Central Terminal
Chrysler Building
Ford Foundation Building
United Nations
Ralph Bunche Plaza
Tudor City
Bryant Park
N.Y. Public Library

Situated by the *East River* is the **United Nations Headquarters**, an iconic part of the New York City skyline. On 1st Avenue stretching from *42nd Street* to *48th Street* covering 18 acres, it is the start of this **PowerHike**. As you approach the four buildings on *1st Avenue*, the alphabetical display of member flags is most impressive. Established in 1945, there are currently 192 member states in this international organization, whose goal is world peace. Nearly every sovereign state, including the Holy See (Vatican), is represented. Because of the global stature of the representatives and the international

nature of the building, be prepared for extensive security and long lines. Tours are

offered Monday – Friday from 9:45 AM – 4:45 PM, in most major languages. It is best to arrive early. You will visit the *General Assembly Hall* (where all member countries participate), as well as other specialized agencies which detail the work of the UN, the *World Health Organization, UNICEF (United Nations Children's Fund*), and the *World Food Program*. Fascinating exhibits, including slide shows

and videos detailing the international work of the ***UN***, are part of the tour. There is awe-inspiring art donated by member countries, such as the *Chagall Stained Glass* depicting symbols of peace and love, the *Norman Rockwell Mosaic*, the *Chinese Ivory Carving*, the *Japanese Peace Bell*, and *The Foucault Pendulum*. The lower public level

of the building has a notable book shop, stamp shop, coffee shop, and several fascinating gift shops carrying items made in different member countries. The garden also has extraordinary sculptures donated by member nations. After the **UN** tour, cross *1st Avenue* at *42nd Street* to ***Ralph Bunche Plaza***. Named after the UN Secretary General, it is a striking slice of green along the busy thoroughfare. Walk around the impressive monument and climb

the stairs to the lookout. It is a good place to appreciate the architectural power of the ***United Nations*** complex as a whole, with the ***East River*** in the background. Walk away from the ***UN*** to the west one block to an unusual residential development called ***Tudor City***. Built on land previously slums, tenements, and slaughterhouses, ***Tudor City*** has its own charming park and enchanting views of the ***East River***. Turn left at the park and wander through this serene green setting. At the other end of *Tudor Park* is a bridge over *42nd Street*. Go down the stairs to the street below. As you walk west on *42nd*

Street, you will pass the ***Ford Foundation Building*** on the right. Go inside to marvel at the 12 story atrium filled with ferns and other tropical plants. Back on *42nd Street*, continue to *Third Avenue*, and the impressive ***Chrysler Building***. It was built in the art deco style by the auto company in 1930. The ornaments on the corners of the building are replicas of Chrysler automobile ornaments. Its gleaming silver spire is emblematic of New York City,

and the landmark is second in height to the ***Empire State Building***. Continue west on *42nd Street* to ***Grand Central Station***, the huge train and subway hub for New York City. It was built in 1913 by William Vanderbilt, son of the railroad magnate Cornelius, who built the first Central Depot in 1871. Enter the vast

Beaux Arts interior known as the *Main Concourse*, from which all the trains

are accessed. Take in the lavish marble walls and floors, then look up to the magnificent ceiling mural of the Mediterranean sky, designed by famous French artist, Paul Helleu. Walk up the elegant marble staircase for a better view of the impressive space and visit *Cipriani Dolci* or *Michael Jordan's The Steakhouse*

N.Y.C. On the lower level take time to explore the collection of specialty shops, markets, restaurants, and the *Transit Museum*. There are weekly guided tours

of historic ***Grand Central Station*** and private tours can also be arranged.

Exit ***Grand Central Station*** onto *Vanderbilt Avenue* and walk to *42nd Street* and *Fifth Avenue* on your way to the ***New York Public Library***. The guardian lions welcome you (nicknamed Patience and Fortitude during the Great Depression) at the entrance stairs. Go up to the third floor and the Reading Room, which is two

blocks long and seats five hundred people. Visit the children's library on the first floor as well. There is a fine shop with unusual books and amusing gifts. Library hours are Monday – Wednesday, 10AM - 8:45 PM: Thursday-Saturday 10AM-5:45PM.

Entrance is free. *Note: If you are visiting around the winter holidays, do not miss the Christmas tree inside the main entrance.*

Just behind the library facing *Avenue of the Americas (Sixth Avenue*) is ***Bryant Park***. The park has a storied history but is now updated and reminiscent of its original French garden design. Currently an "in" spot in town, it has free Wi-Fi and the Southwest Porch near the *Fountain Terrace* where you can relax in an

Adirondack chair. It is the location of the popular *Bryant Park Grill*, *Bryant Park Café*, the

'wichcraft kiosks for coffee, ice cream or lunch, as well as the site of Fashion Week's runway events. *Le Carrousel at Bryant Park* is a treat for all ages, revolving to the tunes of the French cabaret. *The Chess Area* has life size games and *The Pond* is the park's main attraction in the wintertime. The park transforms into an ice rink from November through January. *Celsius* overlooks *The Pond* and offers a special venue for refreshment and *Ice Bites* provides quick snacks. Many public gatherings and performances are held in this vibrant space. Now notice the several historical buildings surrounding the park, especially the distinctive *American Radiator Building*,

which is now the *Bryant Park Hotel*. With its beautiful façade and illuminated gold top, the *Bryant Park Hotel* is one of the city's most distinguished buildings. Across from the park on *40th Street* is the delicious *Lily O'Brien's Chocolate Café*, definitely worth a visit. Return to one of the restaurants in ***Bryant Park*** to relax and reflect on the remarkable buildings you have explored on this exciting ***PowerHike***.

8

SOHO | NOHO | LITTLE ITALY

SoHo

New Museum of Contemporary Art

Guggenheim Museum Soho

NoHo

NoLita

Little Italy

The Italian American Museum

The Tenement Museum

TIME **5–6** hours | **DISTANCE** **5** miles

LOWER
EAST
Side

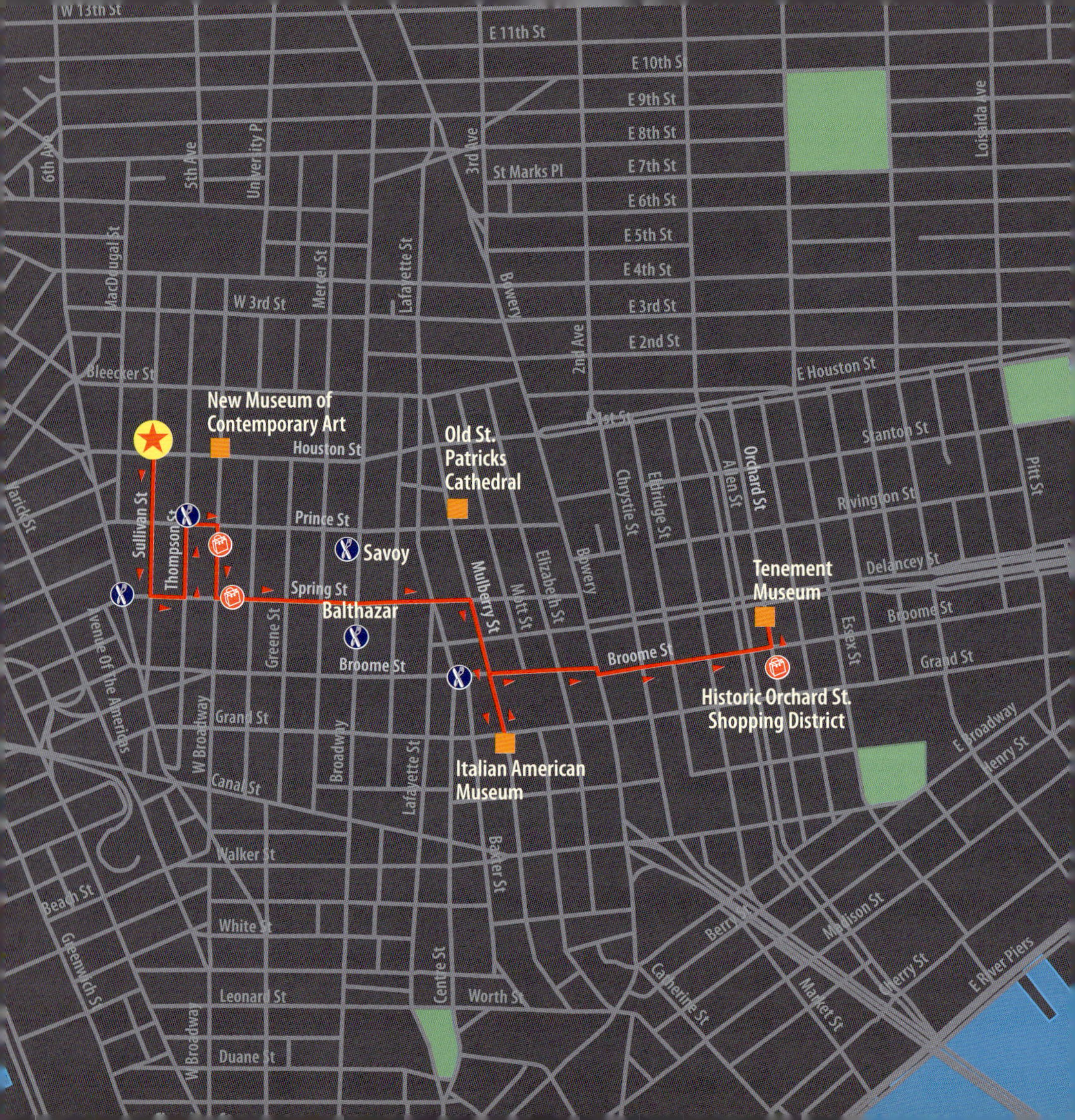
New Museum of Contemporary Art
Old St. Patricks Cathedral
Savoy
Balthazar
Tenement Museum
Historic Orchard St. Shopping District
Italian American Museum
W 13th St
E 11th St
E 10th St
E 9th St
E 8th St
E 7th St
E 6th St
E 5th St
E 4th St
E 3rd St
E 2nd St
St Marks Pl
6th Ave
5th Ave
University Pl
3rd Ave
Loisaida Ave
MacDougal St
Mercer St
Lafayette St
Bowery
2nd Ave
W 3rd St
Bleecker St
E Houston St
Houston St
1st St
Stanton St
Rivington St
Pitt St
Orchard St
Allen St
Eldridge St
Chrystie St
Prince St
Sullivan St
Thompson St
Spring St
Greene St
Mulberry St
Mott St
Elizabeth St
Delancey St
Broome St
Essex St
Grand St
Avenue Of the Americas
W Broadway
Broadway
Canal St
E Broadway
Henry St
Baxter St
Walker St
Beach St
White St
Greenwich St
Leonard St
Worth St
Centre St
Duane St
Berry St
Madison St
Catherine St
Market St
Cherry St
E River Piers

The ***Lower East Side*** of Manhattan Island has been home to immigrants for over 200 years. Squeezed into dense streets teeming with pushcarts, people lived in decrepit tenement buildings under dreadful conditions. In spite of the living conditions, immigrants flocked to New York City and settled in this harsh quarter, struggling to create a new life. On this ***PowerHike*** we explore some of these culturally rich and diverse

neighborhoods as we delve into the melting pot that is New York City. We start with ***SoHo*** and then venture on to ***NoHo, NoLita, Little Italy*** and the

Lower East Side tenements. These neighborhoods are full of history, both in the culture of the immigrants who settled here, as well as in the community that evolved from the blending of these cultures and traditions.

SoHo is known for its cast iron architecture and cobbled streets. In the late 19th century, many buildings were decorated with cast iron facades as a cheap method to create new and interesting structures. Once dark industrial buildings, they became light and expansive factories and warehouses. **SoHo** began to change in the late 1960s as space left empty by departing factories became attractive to artists. High ceilings and light filled space suited lofts and studios and the new character of this neighborhood resulted. It began to attract more affluent residents and became a very

hip place to live and a popular tourist destination. You will find chic shops, restaurants and many tourists. Street vendors line the sidewalks of *Prince Street* and *Spring Street*, as do trendy shops – *Dolce & Gabbana, Prada, H & M, Calvin Klein*. Tourists and New Yorkers alike flock to the area to make the weekend scene. **SoHo** stands for *south of Houston Street* as the heart of the district is found between *Houston Street, West Broadway, Canal Street and Crosby Street*. While expensive boutiques abound, the southern part of **SoHo**, by Canal Street, is the section that reflects its earlier years and tourists come looking for cheap imitations. We start this ***PowerHike*** at the corner of *Houston Street* and *Sullivan Street*. Walk south on *Sullivan Street* noting the historic townhouses and homes that give rise to the character of this neighborhood. Visit local favorites like the *Sullivan Street Bakery* or *Once Upon a Tart* for a quick breakfast treat. One block to the east is *Thompson Street*, another residential jewel. The sidewalks of *Prince Street* and *Spring Street* are filled with street vendors, tourists, and locals in search of the unique creation. This is also a hub for many marvelous little shops and superb cafes. On *Thompson Street* near *Prince Street* is *Cubana Café*. Step into this little outpost of Havana and

enjoy a treat. Famous for its grilled corn, there is always a long line so it is best to visit at off hours. On *Spring Street* near *6th Avenue* are *Aquagrill*, a lively neighborhood spot, and *Balthazar*, at *Crosby Street*, a popular brasserie where brunch starts early and ends late. There is also *Savoy*, a cheerful

rustic inn with a welcoming fireplace. Whatever type of food you desire, from the heartiest European cuisine to a distinctive New York deli sandwich, it can be found in **SoHo**. You will certainly need refreshment after exploring all of the wonderful shops. *West Broadway* is the street known for designers and you can shop *Prada, Dolce &*

Gabbana, Furla, or *Emporio Armani*, just to name a few.

East of *West Broadway* between *Prince Street* and *Houston Street* is the ***New Museum of Contemporary Art***. It is a must visit in this neighborhood. Open after noon each day except Monday and Tuesday, this new structure is an architectural statement and worth a visit if only to gaze at the stunning exterior. There is a café and museum store, as well as the Sky Room where you can enjoy panoramic views of the neighborhood on the weekends. At the corner of *Broadway* and *Prince Street* is the ***Guggenheim Museum SoHo***. Closed on Tuesdays and Wednesdays, this interesting brick structure is worth a visit, although the exhibit is small.

As you cross *Broadway*, to the north is the neighborhood of ***NoHo*** and ***NoLita***, *north of Houston Street* and *north of Little Italy*. Formerly a region of tenements that became a retail and wholesale district, it is now filled with trendy boutiques and restaurants and

is a desirable place to live. Just beyond is *St. Patrick's Cathedral* and early cemetery.

Continue walking out of ***NoHo*** east on *Prince Street* to *Mulberry Street* into the heart of ***Little Italy***. Turn right through the hub of this famous neighborhood. Once crowded with newly arrived Italian families living in tenements, that turn of the century neighborhood is now a profusion of Italian restaurants. If you are visiting in September the annual *Festival*

of San Gennaro with parades and festivities is an event to see. ***The Italian American Museum*** is on the corner of *Mulberry Street* and

Grand Street on the site of the *Banca Stabile*, a bank that provided immigrants financial services as well as serving as a community center and link to relatives in the homeland. The museum is dedicated to maintaining this heritage and there is an interesting exhibit on Italians in New York as well as other appealing

items. Many enticing restaurants await you along the colorful streets. While barkers will encourage you to enter, peruse the entire street and restaurant menus before

deciding. If you are not ready for a hearty Italian meal, visit *Ferrara* for a scrumptious Italian pastry and cappuccino and peek into *Forzanos* to admire the Italian goods. On the corner of *Broome Street,* you will encounter the infamous

neighborhood staple, *Umberto's Clam House.*

Remain on *Broome Street* to *Orchard Street* and the ***Tenement Museum***, a fascinating journey into the past. This *Lower East Side* neighborhood was home to a vast number of immigrants during the 19th and 20th centuries.

Fresh from *Ellis Island* and most not speaking English, they crammed into crowded multiple family buildings seeking solace in their own culture and language. Take a guided tour back in time through one of the authentically restored apartments to gain insight into the rigors of tenement life through artifacts, documents and photos. You can choose a German-Jewish or Italian family, a Jewish family and garment shop, or an Irish family. Without indoor plumbing, electricity or gas heat, life in the teeming tenements was extremely harsh for those trying to forge a new life. This tour will leave a lasting impression. For unique souvenirs, the Museum Shop offers a superb selection of books and New York gifts. (Since tours are very popular and limited to small groups, it is wise to purchase tickets in advance online or by telephone.)

After such a full day, you will want to relax and partake in the nightlife of one of

these *Lower East Side* neighborhoods. There are so many exciting and delicious restaurants and cafes to choose from. Sit down in one of these colorful New York neighborhoods and enjoy another memorable New York meal as you recall the unique blend of history and culture experienced in today's ***PowerHike***.

9 THE RIVERS OF MANHATTAN

Hudson River

Battery Park

Statue of Liberty

Ellis Island

East River

Brooklyn Bridge

Manhattan Bridge

Queensboro Bridge

Harlem River

USS Intrepid

The West 79th Street Boat Basin Café

Riverside Park

Children's Museum

Café Lalo

TIME **1** hour | **DISTANCE** **3** miles

walking plus boat trip

CENTRAL PARK
Detail Area
Queensboro Bridge
Queens Midtown Tunnel
Circle Line Boats
Intrepid
Williamsburg Bridg
Holland Tunnel
River Cafe
Governor Nelson A Rockefeller Park
Manhattan Bridge
Brooklyn Bridge
Liberty

Riverside Park South
Riverside Dr
Children's Museum
Cafe Lalo
W 86th St
W 85th St
W 83rd St
W 81st St
Boat Basin Cafe
79th St Boat Basin
W 79th St
W 77th St
W 75th St
W 73rd St
W 72nd St
Broadway
West End Ave
W 69th St
W 66th St
W 65th St
W 64th St
8th Ave
Park Dr S
Amsterdam Ave
W 59th St
W 58th St
W 57th St
W 55th St
De Witt Clinton Park
W 53rd St
W 51st St
12th Ave
11th Ave
9th Ave
W 49th St
W 47th St
Intrepid
W 45th St
10th Ave
W 43rd St
W 42nd St
W 41st St
Circle Line
W 39th St

While the first thought of Manhattan is hustle and bustle and concrete jungle, the amazing beauty of New York City is its waterways. The borough of Manhattan is an island surrounded on the west by the *Hudson River*, on the south by *New York Harbor*, on the east by the *East River*, and on the north by the *Harlem River*. The rivers are a special way to get a unique perspective of Manhattan, terrific photographs, and spectacular views. They are the perfect location to begin sightseeing in New York and a not-to-be-missed adventure.

This ***PowerHike*** starts on the ***Hudson River*** at ***Pier 83*** at *42nd Street*. After purchasing tickets (it can be done online in advance) board one of the *Circle Line*

boats for your water adventure. The boat trips range from one hour to three hours and are a perfectly delightful way to see the skyline, learn a little about the city, or see the lights of the city on an evening cruise. Whether you choose the conventional ferry ride, an evening music cruise, or the Beast, a thrilling speedboat ride, you are in for a treat. The tour guide on the boat is quite informative and provides you with historical and comical facts about the stunning panorama before you. As you venture out, the boat passes huge buildings housing fans providing air to the ***Holland Tunnel***,

Rockefeller Park, ***Battery City Park*** and the financial district, all with sweeping views of the immense buildings that make up the city skyline. Sailing past the ***Statue of Liberty***, the ***Verrazano Bridge*** and entrance to New York Harbor appear in the distance. Thoughts cannot help but turn to the many who sailed under the bridge for the first time on their way to a new future in a new country. Turning up the ***East River*** you pass by the ***South Street Seaport***, under the ***Brooklyn Bridge***, and the ***Manhattan Bridge*** while glimpsing the borough of Brooklyn on the right. Look carefully

for *The River Cafe*, a small but very elegant restaurant with magical skyline views. At *Roosevelt Island* the boat sails under the *Queensboro* or ***59th Street Bridge***. There is a unique restaurant and nightclub, *Gustavino*, built inside the base of the bridge. As you

approach the Bronx, the boat veers to the left onto the ***Harlem River*** and sails past the upper part of Manhattan. Passing under the ***Henry Hudson Bridge*** you return to the ***Hudson River*** and sail south to return to ***Pier 83***. At the end of your cruise and now a seasoned Manhattan adventurer, you will want to see more and now know

the locations that you want to explore on other ***PowerHikes***.

As you disembark from your island tour, walk left towards the huge aircraft carrier in front of you. ***The USS Intrepid*** saw battle in World War II, the Korean War, and the Vietnam War. It is now an historical landmark and a sea, air and space museum. With many interactive exhibits, the ship is open for tours daily and is a truly remarkable experience.

Continue walking uptown along the ***Riverwalk.*** The City of New York has made extensive improvements to this walkway and you will see New Yorkers everywhere enjoying the beautiful areas

along the water. There are parks, cafes, playgrounds, flowers, views, kayaks and boats for rent. Old docks have become beautiful parks and the grass stretches out into the river creating an amazingly tranquil setting in this very busy city. Venture out onto these piers for unparalleled views of the ***Hudson River***. The ***Riverwalk*** is a strikingly attractive and much used recreational area. As you approach *79th Street* and ***Riverside Park***, you see the

79th Street Boat Basin, a marina at **Riverside Park**. It

is the only marina in New York City where New Yorkers can actually live on their boats. There is also a wonderful restaurant, open during the summer months, the *West 79th Street Boat Basin Café*, in an open-air, tiled rotunda. Located right on the water, the views of the river and New Jersey are amazing and it is a unique atmosphere – a perfect spot to relax, take in the scenery, and view a spectacular sunset.

Once you are refreshed, cross *Riverside Drive* to *83rd Street*. Walk east towards *Amsterdam Avenue*, passing the **Children's Museum** on the right, to **Café**

Lalo, your destination across the street. ***Café Lalo*** is a charming, European style, open-air restaurant with delicious food and scrumptious desserts. It is casual and relaxed and well known among

New Yorkers as a special place before and after theater. Famous for its part in the movie, *You've Got Mail*, and with its twinkling lights outside, it is a perfect site to enjoy New York and reflect on this amazing day. If energy permits, you can continue on and take in the theater and an even later supper at the famous theater district restaurant, *Joe Allen*. Remember, New York is "the city that never sleeps!"

10 CENTRAL PARK SOUTH

Grand Army Plaza

Pulitzer Fountain

Plaza Hotel

Central Park

Columbus Circle

Time Warner Center

Museum of Art and Design

Carnegie Hall

Times Square

Theater District

TIME 4–5 hours | **DISTANCE** 5 miles

MILLENN
Pepsi-Cola
POP
refresheverything.com
LOVETC.
JOY
WHO IS
THE HOTTEST GIRL ON THE PLANET?
THE GUY OF THE YEAR?
THE MOST DANGEROUS MAN?
GUYS CHOICE
SUNDAY JUNE 21
1500
swatch
swatch
swatch+ swatch+
WHO IS

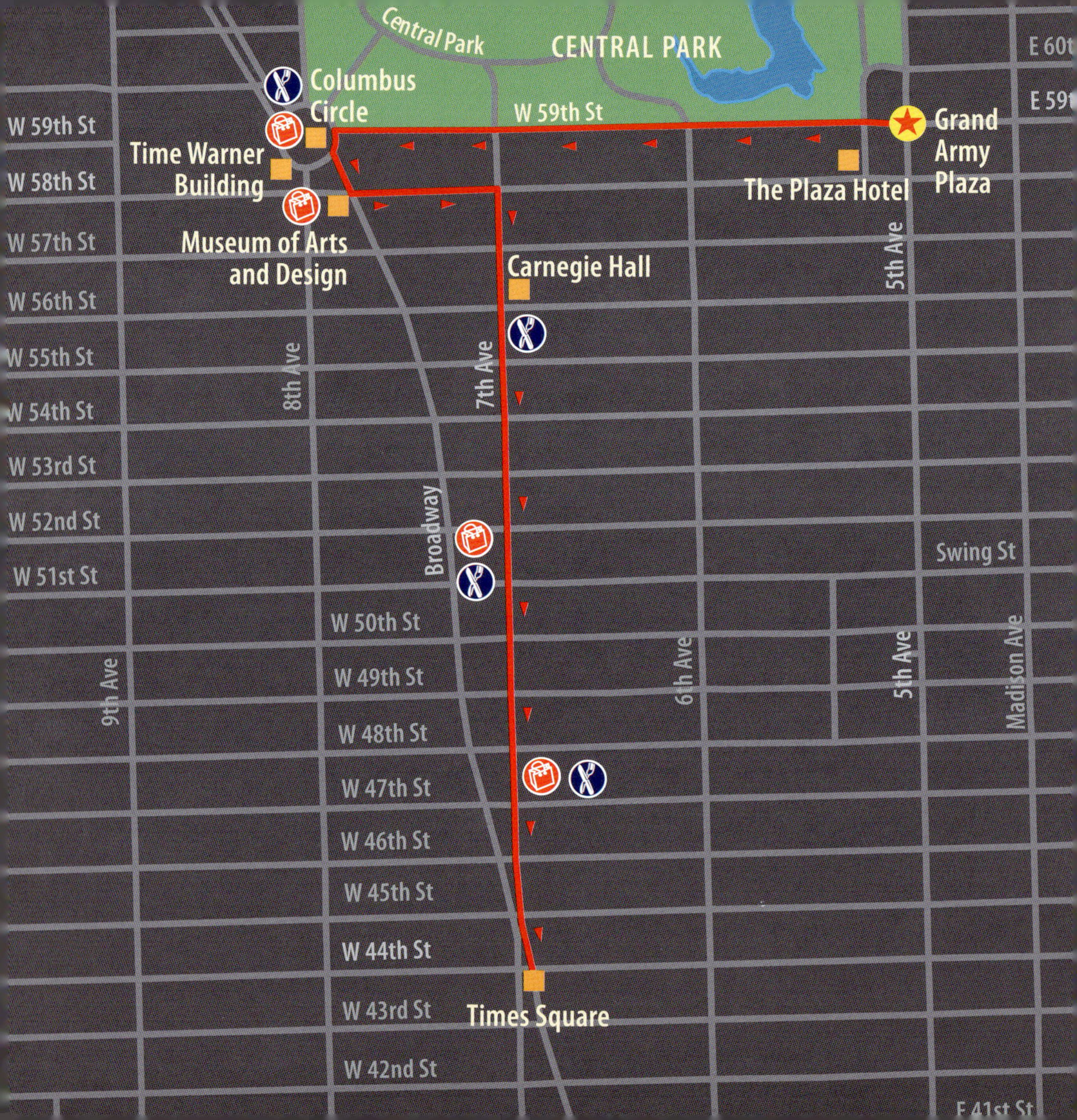

CENTRAL PARK
Central Park
Columbus Circle
Time Warner Building
Museum of Arts and Design
Carnegie Hall
The Plaza Hotel
Grand Army Plaza
Times Square
W 59th St
W 58th St
W 57th St
W 56th St
W 55th St
W 54th St
W 53rd St
W 52nd St
W 51st St
W 50th St
W 49th St
W 48th St
W 47th St
W 46th St
W 45th St
W 44th St
W 43rd St
W 42nd St
Swing St
9th Ave
8th Ave
Broadway
7th Ave
6th Ave
5th Ave
Madison Ave

Central Park, Fifth Avenue, the Plaza Hotel, Times Square, Broadway, Time Warner Center, all are synonymous with the excitement and energy of the City of New York.

This ***PowerHike*** takes us through this electrifying and vibrant part of the city and it should be experienced both in daytime and at night as New York City is "the city that never sleeps". We begin at ***Grand Army Plaza*** at the corner of *Fifth Avenue* and *59th Street* or *Central Park South*. The beautiful fountain across from the *Sherman Monument* at the entrance to *Central Park* is the ***Pulitzer Fountain***,

built with funds donated by Joseph Pulitzer. Across the street are the flags and grand entrance of the celebrated ***Plaza Hotel***. We visit ***The Plaza*** on the ***Fifth Avenue PowerHike***, but do wander through its beautiful portal to look around.

Walk west on *Central Park South*, passing the picturesque street vendors selling everything from photos and drawings to warm nuts and hot dogs. You also pass the famous horse carriages lined up along the street. What fun to take a ride through

Central Park in a carriage! At *Sixth Avenue* or *Avenue of the Americas*, continue past the ***Artists' Gate*** entrance to **Central Park** and beyond *Seventh Avenue* to

Columbus Circle. ***Columbus Circle*** marks the intersection of *Broadway, Central Park West, Central Park South*, and *Eighth Avenue*. There is a beautifully lit statue and fountain, surrounded by

gorgeous flowers, named after Christopher Columbus, and made famous in such movies as *The Devil Wears Prada* and *Home Alone 2.* This circle is particularly enchanting at night. Walk around it to ***Time Warner Center***, one of the newest architectural masterpieces in the city. ***Time Warner Center*** has it all: Time Warner World *Headquarters, CNN New York* headquarters, *The Shops at Columbus Circle*, *The Mandarin Oriental Hotel*, luxury condos, and several gourmet restaurants. *The Shops at Columbus Circle* are a destination of exciting retailers. From clothing to jewelry, cosmetics to fine gifts, cigars and chocolate, you can find whatever you need. There is a fitness club, a bookstore featuring the *Dean & Deluca Café*, and on the lower level is *Whole Foods Market*, a must visit. It has 59,000 square feet of delectable natural, organic and unique foods. Wander the aisles and marvel at this truly magnificent market. The restaurant scene at ***Time Warner Center*** is

also a must see. With several venues to choose from, it is a location to return to several times. Thomas Keller's *Per Se* is a strikingly beautiful restaurant with sweeping views of **Columbus Circle**, *59th Street* and beyond. There is also *Landmarc, Porterhouse New York, Masa*, and *Barmasa*. All are very popular and reservations are recommended. For a simple meal there is *Bouchon Bakery* and for a high energy evening with spectacular views there is *Stone Rose Lounge*. ***Time Warner Center*** is a ***PowerHike*** in its own right so allow plenty of time to explore. With is proximity to ***Central Park***, it is also a destination for meals following the two *Central Park* **PowerHikes**.

Exit the huge glass doors to *59th Street* and follow the circle to the right to the ***Museum of Art and Design*** at *2 Columbus Circle*. Open Tuesday through Sunday, there are tours available of the fascinating exhibitions and collections. On the ground floor is the store with unique one of a kind items. Continue on *59th Street* to *Seventh Avenue*, and turn right towards ***Times Square***. As you approach the corner of *57th Street* you will see the world famous ***Carnegie Hall***. Renowned for its acoustics and built by philanthropist Andrew Carnegie in 1891, ***Carnegie Hall*** is New York City's most famous venue for concerts and music. There are actually three performance spaces, the *Main Hall* or *Isaac Stern Auditorium*, and two smaller venues. There are docent led tours of the hall and auditoriums as well as a shop with books, music and distinctive memorabilia. Should you be hungry, there is the *Citi Café, Parterre Bar, Jacobs Room*, and private banquet facilities. The *Rose Museum* has a fascinating exhibit of the history of ***Carnegie Hall*** and the artists who have performed within its walls.

Hours vary so check the web site. *57th Street* is the location of many shops and restaurants such as the *Brooklyn Diner, Europa Café* and French bistro, *Rue 57*. Continue walking along *7th Avenue* passing New York eateries such as *Lindy's* (famous for cheesecake) and *Carnegie Deli*, family owned since 1937 and a city landmark, visited by celebrities for the famous pastrami and corned beef sandwiches and astoundingly large pieces of cheesecake. Autographed caricatures

of the personalities line the walls of the deli.

You will also pass *Trattoria d'Arte, Carmines* (featuring large quantities of family style Italian food), *Maison, Bond 45* and *Redeye*. Choose one of these typical New York eateries and relax before a visit to a ***Times Square*** theater.

As you approach

Times Square – world famous symbol of the city, neon lights and marquees, and giant electronic and digital signs, all come into view.

Through great effort and redevelopment on the part of the city, it is tourist friendly and increasingly upscale. Thousands of people enjoy the scene day and night. The sidewalks are always crowded and the city is currently experimenting with the idea of a pedestrian mall between *42nd* and *47th Streets.*

Imagine people sitting in beach chairs in the middle of the street! ***Times Square*** is where *Broadway* joins *7th Avenue* and the location of the famous crystal ball which descends to usher in each New Year, a tradition started in 1907. There are jumbotrons where you can follow NASDAQ or the weather. There are advertisements, a giant movie complex, restaurants, stores, hotels, theaters, and enormous billboards advertising the Broadway shows. This is truly the heartbeat of New York City, its most lively area.

The famous ***New York Theater District*** and Broadway surround ***Times Square*** between *40th* and *54th Streets*. The ***Theater District*** was once called "The Great White Way" because of the many lights on billboards and marquees. It is a major tourist venue and another symbol of the vibrancy of New York City. There will certainly be a show to please everyone and attending a Broadway show is part of a visit to New York. Following a show, indulge in one of the many ***Theater District*** eateries such as *Charley O's, Center Stage Café*, *District, Gallagher's Steak House, Joe Allen Restaurant, Rosie O'*

Grady's, or *Sardi's*, legendary choice of stars after the theater, its walls covered

with caricatures of Broadway's and Hollywood's most famous. Choose any one of the many fun locales to enjoy or return to one of the hot spots at **Columbus Circle** and enjoy New York City at night.

11

UPPER WEST SIDE

Central Park

The Dakota

Strawberry Fields

New York Historical Society Museum

American Museum of Natural History

Rose Center For Earth And Space and the Hayden Planetarium

Theodore Roosevelt Park

The Lincoln Center for the Performing Arts

TIME All Day | **DISTANCE** **6** miles

UPPER WEST SIDE
Riverside Dr
W 86th St
W 85th St
Transverse Rd
85th St
E 85th St
E 84th St
W End Ave
Theodore Roosevelt Park
Zabar's
W 80th St
Hayden Planetarium
Turtle Pond
East Dr
E 79th St
American Museum Of Natural History
79th Transverse Rd
W 77th St
Amsterdam Ave
New York Historical Society
CENTRAL PARK
Madison Ave
Park Ave
The Lake
W 73rd St
Henry Hudson Pky
W 72nd St
The Dakota
Imagine
E 72nd St
Terrace Dr
Broadway
Central Park W
Center Dr
West End Ave
W 67th St
W 66th St
W 65th St
W 64th St
East Dr
E 66th St
E 65th St
65th St
Julliard School
Lincoln Center
Damrosch Park
Fordham University
Joe DiMaggio Hwy
West Dr
5th Ave
The Pond
W 60th St
E 60th St
E 59th St
Columbus Circle
9th Ave
8th Ave
7th Ave

The ***Upper West Side*** is a dynamic neighborhood located between the ***Hudson River*** and ***Central Park***. Along with its elegant brownstone townhouses and quiet tree-lined streets, the residents enjoy ***Central Park*** as their backyard, playground, and refuge from the fast pace of urban life in New York City. ***Lincoln Center for the Performing Arts*** is only a short walk away, and there are great restaurants and shopping in that direction, as well as in the ***Time Warner Building*** at ***Columbus Circle*** just beyond ***Lincoln Center***.

The American Museum of Natural History*, *The Rose Center For Earth And Space, *the* ***Hayden Planetarium***, and the ***New York Historical Society Museum,*** are world-class institutions of culture and learning. At the northernmost reaches of the ***Upper West Side*** are *Barnard College, Columbia University*, and the *Manhattan School of Music*. These institutions and eclectic residents make the ***Upper West Side*** a destination full of power, energy, and fun.

While this vibrant neighborhood can be reached along the pathways bordering the west side of *Central Park*, this ***PowerHike*** walks uptown on tree-lined *Central Park West*. Along *Central Park West* you pass many buildings considered to be some of the most desirable places to live in Manhattan. One of the most famous

of these residences is ***The Dakota***, at *72nd Street* and *Central Park West*. It was built between 1880 and 1884, in the German Renaissance style and, at the time, was a new concept in residential life for the upper class of Manhattan. They had always lived in large single-family residences and ***The Dakota*** is a building of enormous apartments. The apartments are glorious and offer all the amenities of the New Yorker's lifestyle. There are 65 residences, featuring 14 foot ceilings and vast rooms overlooking ***Central Park***, as well as a beautiful central courtyard. ***The Dakota*** and similar residence buildings along *Central Park West* soon became very popular and a desired location to live. Many famous people reside in and have resided in ***The Dakota***, one being *Beatle*, John Lennon, who tragically was shot in front of the entrance. Just across from ***The Dakota***, inside ***Central Park***, is the memorial to Lennon, ***Imagine***, a large black and white mosaic circle. Crowds of people from all over the world visit the memorial and it is a favorite destination of tour groups. Visiting early is a way to avoid the crowds.

At *77th Street* and *Central Park West* is the ***New York Historical Society Museum***. It is the oldest museum in New York City, well known as a research

library and educational institution. The museum features the history of New York and its people, the founding of our country, the history of art in America, and chronicles American culture up to the present time. It is celebrated for its collection of the Hudson River School and the American Romantics. John James Audubon's watercolors for *Birds of America* and decorative arts pieces such as their Tiffany lamp collection are popular exhibits and the historical artifact exhibit is not to be missed. There are also

temporary exhibitions such as ***Lincoln and New York, Dutch New York,*** and ***John Brown: The Abolitionist and His Legacy.*** The library reading room is particularly beautiful and has a very special stained glass window. As a major research institution, the library is a center of activity. The library is closed Sunday and Monday, the museum only on Monday. Visit the interesting museum shop full of historical artifacts and also the delightful *Café at N-YHS*.

Continue up *Central Park West* to *79th Street*, and one of New York City's most exciting museums, the ***American Museum of Natural History and the Rose***

Center for Earth and Space and the Hayden Planetarium. This amazing complex contains archeology, anthropology, geology, dinosaurs, a butterfly conservatory, and fascinating temporary exhibits. This is an excellent museum for families and there is much to see so allow plenty of time. The museum is open daily (a perfect place to explore on Mondays when the other museums are closed) from 10AM - 5:45PM. Advance tickets are available online, or you can use the extremely helpful New York City Pass (info at www.newyorkpass.com). The museum gift shops are extraordinary in the quality and quantity of educational material available. The *Museum Food Court* is on the lower level and the *Starlight Café* is located on the first level.

The Rose Center For Earth And Space can be entered from within the ***American Museum of Natural History***. It is a particularly exciting museum and the space show in the *Hayden Planetarium* is especially thrilling. A walk around the *Heilbrunn Cosmic Pathway* is an education in itself. Tickets are required for the space show. Exit the museum through the planetarium on *81st Street* into ***Theodore Roosevelt Park***. It is a vision of flowers, pathways, and serenity. Enjoy it and

relax before venturing on to the busier part of the neighborhood.

Walk south or downtown on *Columbus Avenue*. At *80th Street* turn right to Broadway and *Zabar's*, an "only in New York" foodie emporium selling gourmet foods such as cheese and caviar as well as huge bins of coffee beans from all over the world. Every inch of this store is filled with food and the most amazing kitchen items. They will even ship their famous New York toasting bagels for you! Shopping on Broadway is fun – all the usual upscale stores are present, and there are plenty of cafes and restaurants, pet stores and even a pet spa!

Continue downtown on *Broadway* and ***The Lincoln Center for the Performing Arts*** looms ahead at *62nd Street*. This spectacular campus houses venues for theater, ballet, opera, and the Philharmonic. *The Juilliard School* is adjacent, as is *Fordham University*. The idea of the center was conceived in the 1950s as part of slum renovation under the leadership of John D. Rockefeller III. One by one

the various artistic organizations in New York, such as the Philharmonic, the Opera, and the Ballet, joined the initiative and construction began in the 60s. Improvements have continued to the present. ***Lincoln Center*** is a glittering monument to the artistic soul of New Yorkers. Do plan to attend a performance. There are concerts, dance, opera, theater, film, and jazz, all performed in this magnificent setting and the lights and fountains at night are quite special. It will be an unforgettable experience,

and the best of New York nightlife. The *Center* has several venues for refreshment, *at 65, Arpeggio Food and Wine*, and the *Grand Tier Restaurant*, but there are also a number of neighborhood restaurants along *Broadway* and *Columbus Avenue*, most with delightful sidewalk settings. For dinner before, or in the Manhattan style, after the performance, try one and enjoy the surrounding neighborhood. *Café Fiorello* is always a favorite and a perfect site to reflect on this amazing ***PowerHike*** and the incredible culture and energy of New York City's ***Upper West Side***.

12 THE HIGH LINE

The High Line

Hudson River

Chelsea

Chelsea Piers Sports & Entertainment Complex

Meatpacking District

TIME **4–5** hours | **DISTANCE** **3** miles

W 27th St
W 26th St
W 25th St
W 24th St
W 23rd St
W 22nd St
W 21st St
W 20th St
W 19th St
W 18th St
W 17th St
W 16th St
W 15th St
W 14th St
W 12th St
W 11th St
W 10th St
N River Piers
10th Ave
High Line
Empire Diner
CHELSEA
Chelsea Pier
11th Ave
9th Ave
8th Ave
7th Ave
Chelsea Market
MEATPACKING DISTRICT
Washington St
Hudson St
High Line
Gansevoort
Horatio St
Jane St
Bank St
Perry St

Manhattan Island, colossal metropolis with towering buildings and crowds of people, also celebrates parks and oases of greenery throughout the city. Manhattan's newest oasis of green is a unique and extraordinary park. On the northwest side of *Greenwich Village* is ***The High Line***. Where elevated train lines used to run, there is now a glorious linear *greenway* high above the city streets. Take a walk on ***The High Line*** into the history of this formerly industrial neighborhood. In the 1930s train tracks were elevated above the city to reduce the number of accidents between people and the freight trains bringing

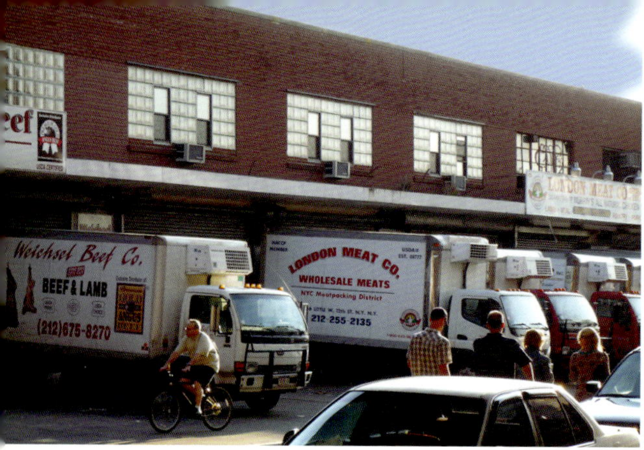

goods to the warehouses and factories in this locale. Rising above what is known as the **Meatpacking District**, the trains brought meat and other goods to the warehouses located on the streets below. Used into the 1980s, the trains gradually became obsolete as trucks carried more and more of the freight. People began to clamor for demolition of the railway line and, in the 1990s, Friends of the High Line was formed to promote preservation of the history of the district and use of the railway as public open space. In 2006, after much interaction with the city, work began on the remarkable project creating a park from the elevated train line. In June 2009 the first section of ***The High Line***, *Gansevoort Street* to *20th Street*, opened

for people to enjoy. Ultimately it will extend a mile and a half through the *Meatpacking District*, *Chelsea* and *Clinton/Hell's Kitchen* to *34th Street,* and is open daily from 7 AM to 10 PM.

Enter this astonishing *park in the sky* and begin this unique **PowerHike** at the *Gansevoort Stair*. It offers visitors views of the city and the *Hudson River* in a very natural setting. Old railroad ties remain and

much of the landscaping is created from weeds and wild growth on the unused tracks. A gravel pathway meanders along and benches and chaise lounges made from sustainable forests are built in along the way. Trees have been planted to provide shade. There is an historic tour that you can follow, and the map and audio can be downloaded from ***The High Line*** web site. Just before reaching

W. 13th Street is ***The Standard***, a distinctive hotel built over ***The High Line***. It is a popular spot with *The Standard Grill,* a favorite for brunch, located under ***The High Line***, the outdoor *Biergarten* next to it and *The Living Room* featuring live music.

Descend from ***The High Line*** at *20th Street* into ***Chelsea***. This hip neighborhood is well known for its art galleries and

studios. To the west is the ***Chelsea Piers Sports & Entertainment Complex***. This waterfront village is located between *17th Street and 23rd Street* on the *Hudson River* and was constructed on neglected, dilapidated piers. Where luxury liners once docked there is now a fabulous sporting venue, amazing in its scope of waterfront recreation for the city. The Sky Rink provides hockey and skating, the Field House offers

basketball, soccer, rock climbing and camps; and there is a health club, golf club, child care, bowling, sports bar, sports training, The Spa at Chelsea Piers, event venues, as well as restaurants and boating services. There is even Silver Screen Studios, one of the centers of Manhattan's television and film production. Walk west to *11th Avenue* to see this amazing venue. What wonderful uses the city of New York has made of its shorelines

and waterways.

Retrace your steps back up *20th Street* dropping in on galleries as you go. At *22nd Street and 10th Avenue* is the *Empire Diner*, distinctive in its style and made famous in movies. At *Ninth Avenue,* walk uptown to 23rd Street and right along this delightful street of brownstone houses. You pass the *Hotel Chelsea* which was built in 1883 as apartment cooperatives and became a hotel in1905. Listed on the National Register of Historic Places and architecturally famous, the hotel was home to many artists, poets and musicians, including Dylan Thomas.

Some survivors of the *Titanic* lived there briefly as well.

Return to *20th Street* and **The High Line** and stroll back to *14th Street,* and the center of the **Meatpacking District**. This historic neighborhood was home to the open air *Gansevoort Market* in the late 19th century and then to slaughterhouses and meatpacking warehouses. In the 1990s a transformation began and it became

hip and fashionable as chic boutiques opened and the restaurant and night club scene made it the place to be. On *Ninth Avenue* between *15th* and *16th Streets* is the *Chelsea Market*. Located where the National Biscuit Company once produced animal crackers and Oreo cookies, it is now an array of stores and restaurants and is the largest collection of gourmet shops in the city. Both the *Fat Witch Bakery* and *Sarabeth's Bakery* are worth a visit for unusual and delectable sweets. Also on *Ninth Avenue*

is the *Gansevoort Hotel*, a popular site with its rooftop pool and *Plunge Rooftop Bar*, a busy and vibrant scene with fantastic views. There are several fun restaurants to choose from: *Pastis, the Buddha Bar, Son Cubano, Spice Market, SKT*, and clubs such as *PM* and *Cielo*. All will be crowded and reservations are advised, but worth the adventure as you enjoy another gastronomic treat in one of Manhattan's new and lively neighborhoods – the perfect ending to a unique and unusual ***PowerHike***.

13

UPTOWN

Fort Tryon Park

The Cloisters

Columbia University

Uptown Broadway

Cathedral Church of Saint John the Divine

Morningside Park

TIME **4** hours | **DISTANCE**

Fort Tryon and The Cloisters **2+** miles
Columbia University **1+** miles
Saint John the Divine, Morningside Park, Amsterdam **2** miles
Walk back to midtown **13** blocks

Inwood Hill Park
Cooper St
Dyckman St
Vermilyea Ave
Riverside Dr
Park Dr
Sherman Ave
The Cloisters
Ellwood St
Nagle Ave
Margaret Corbin Dr
Fort Tryon Park
Hillside Ave
Fort Washington Park
Riverside Dr
Bennett Ave

W 123rd St
Morningside Dr
W 120th St
Low Memorial Library
St. Paul's Chapel
Low Plaza
College Walk
Morningside Park
Morningside Ave
COLUMBIA UNIVERSITY
Amsterdam Ave
Butler Library
Tom's Restaurant
W 114th St
W 113th St
Broadway
Cathedral of St. John the Divine
W 112th St
W 111th St
Amsterdam Ave
W 110th St
W 109th St
W 108th St
W 107th St
W 106th St

At the northwest tip of the island of Manhattan, beyond the hustle and bustle of midtown, sits beautiful **Fort Tryon**. This serene and peaceful setting overlooking the *Hudson River* is the first destination in the exploration of the uptown part of the island. The **PowerHike** begins on the subway. Take the **A** train uptown and get off at *190th Street*. Follow the directions up the elevator and exit onto *Fort Washington Avenue*. Turn right to *Margaret Corbin Circle* and follow *Margaret Corbin Drive* into the park. **Fort Tryon Park** is a natural woodland of rocks and

vine covered cliffs, bordered by lush lawns, specimen trees, breathtaking vistas, and seasonal flowers. There are a myriad of paths to follow through magnificent trees with stunning views over the *Hudson River*. You can watch the boat traffic on the river and the Fort is home to many species of birds and a perfect spot to watch the Atlantic migration. It is a setting to be enjoyed through all the seasons, as the wildlife and flowers change throughout the year. Not to be missed is the *Heather Garden*, known as the jewel of the park. ***Fort Tryon Park*** is an historic treasure as well. First inhabited in the 1600s and the site of a major Revolutionary War battle, large estates were built there during the 1800s. The land was purchased in 1917 by John D. Rockefeller, who created the park.

Follow *Mary Corbin Drive*, passing

the *New Leaf Café* and the plaque memorializing the Revolutionary battle and Mary Corbin, up the hill to ***The Cloisters***. ***The Cloisters*** is a museum and gardens and a branch of the *Metropolitan Museum of Art*. It is open daily except Mondays from 9:30 AM to 5:15 PM. Situated on the top of a hill with spectacular views of ***Fort Tryon Park*** and the *Hudson River*, ***The Cloisters*** was built by John D. Rockefeller. It is designed

as a medieval building and houses works of art from the Middle Ages, with many original architectural details brought over from Europe and incorporated into the building itself, displayed as they might have been at the time. Exhibited at ***The Cloisters*** are the famous Unicorn Tapestries from Brussels woven in the 1500s. The gardens are famous in their own right and all are designed as cloisters or

retreats for meditation. *The Trie Café*, a peaceful spot for a snack, is located in one of the beautiful cloister gardens planted with European flowers and herbs. There is a very nice bookstore and gift shop that is well worth a visit. With its unique location and castle-like appearance, ***The Cloisters*** is an exceptionally special place to visit. Upon leaving ***The Cloisters*** and ***Fort Tryon Park***, return to the subway and take the **A** train towards downtown to *168th Street*. Switch to the ***No. 1*** train

heading downtown and get off at *116th Street*. You will be in the neighborhood known as *Morningside Heights* and at the main gates of ***Columbia University*** where our ***PowerHike*** continues. Pass through the impressive gates and onto the campus grounds. Founded as King's College in 1754, it is New York State's oldest university. Originally holding classes in a schoolhouse next to Trinity Church downtown, King's College became Columbia College following the Revolutionary

War. In 1896 it became Columbia University and, after four moves, found its permanent home uptown in 1897. The campus today stretches from *110th Street* to *122nd Street* and from *Riverside Drive* to *Morningside Park*.

Once inside the campus, it is hard to imagine that you are in the middle of Manhattan as the campus is an oasis of tranquility and beauty in the busy city. ***PowerHike*** along *College Walk* and you will see *Low Memorial Library*, a landmark building of classical architecture, on the left and, across *Low Plaza*, *Butler Library*. Take your time wandering around campus, passing the new student center, residence halls (most students live on campus) and classroom buildings, many of which are registered as historical buildings. Be sure to see the beautiful *St Paul's Chapel* and cross the campus bridge over *Amsterdam Street*. The medical center, sports facilities and several laboratories reside in other parts of the city.

Return to the main gate and exit onto Broadway turning left toward downtown. You will pass many fun bistros, cafes and restaurants, such as *Le Monde Brasserie*, on your way to *Tom's Restaurant* at *112th Street*. A favorite in the community and serving hearty American food, Tom's is best known as the local diner in the TV series, *Seinfeld*. Turn left at *112th Street* and walk one block to *Amsterdam* and the **Cathedral Church of Saint John the Divine**. Founded in 1882, the cathedral has a storied history. Spend some time inside as well as in the beautiful

gardens. It is open to visitors daily. There are tours available and you may be lucky enough to be there during one of the organ concerts. Behind the cathedral is *Morningside Drive* where the lovely **Morningside Park** begins. It stretches to *123rd Street* and is worth a side trip to see the beautiful trees, waterfall and pond, or retrace your steps to *Tom's Restaurant* or one of the many other interesting local establishments.

Re-board the subway at *110th* and *Broadway* and take the **No. 1** train downtown to *72nd Street*. Go east one block to *Amsterdam* and you will find a charming neighborhood with a number of delightful restaurants and shops within a block in either direction of *Amsterdam* and *72nd*. It is a perfect location to relax and reflect on your morning. From here it is an easy subway ride on the **No. 1** train towards downtown back to midtown, or, better yet, continue your ***PowerHike*** down *Amsterdam* or *Broadway* to midtown.

14

MANHATTAN A LA CARTE

Greenwich Village

Washington Square

Union Square

Flatiron Building

Penn Station

Madison Square Garden

7th Avenue Fashion Avenue

Fashion Institute of Technology

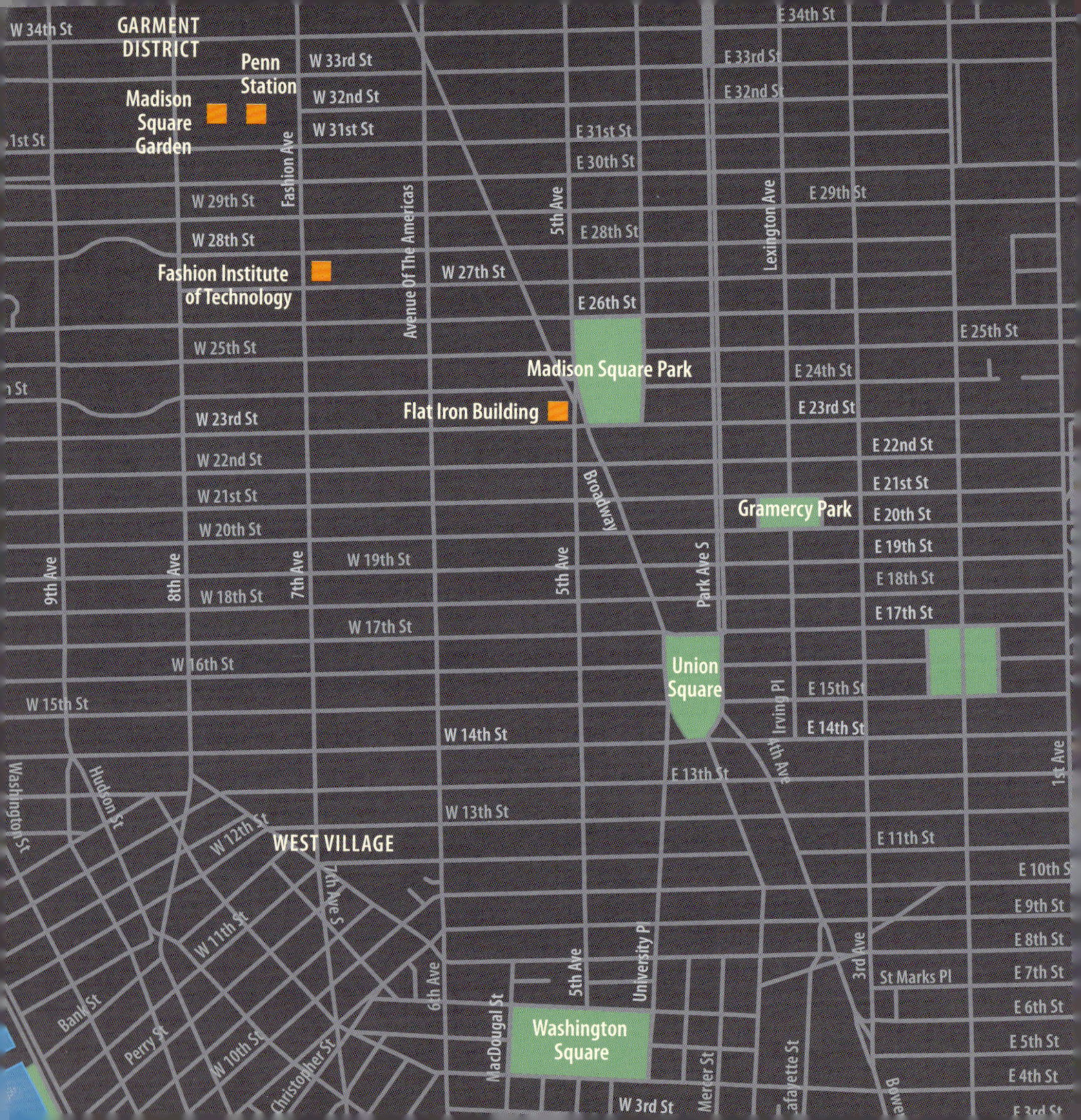
GARMENT DISTRICT
Penn Station
Madison Square Garden
Fashion Institute of Technology
Madison Square Park
Flat Iron Building
Gramercy Park
Union Square
WEST VILLAGE
Washington Square
W 34th St
W 33rd St
W 32nd St
W 31st St
W 29th St
W 28th St
W 27th St
W 25th St
W 23rd St
W 22nd St
W 21st St
W 20th St
W 19th St
W 18th St
W 17th St
W 16th St
W 15th St
W 14th St
W 13th St
W 12th St
W 11th St
W 10th St
W 3rd St
E 34th St
E 33rd St
E 32nd St
E 31st St
E 30th St
E 29th St
E 28th St
E 26th St
E 25th St
E 24th St
E 23rd St
E 22nd St
E 21st St
E 20th St
E 19th St
E 18th St
E 17th St
E 15th St
E 14th St
E 13th St
E 11th St
E 9th St
E 8th St
E 7th St
E 6th St
E 5th St
E 4th St
St Marks Pl
Fashion Ave
Avenue Of The Americas
5th Ave
Lexington Ave
Broadway
Park Ave S
Irving Pl
9th Ave
8th Ave
7th Ave
Washington St
Hudson St
7th Ave S
6th Ave
MacDougal St
University Pl
Mercer St
3rd Ave
1st Ave
Bank St
Perry St
Christopher St

Greenwich Village

Washington Square

Union Square

Flatiron Building

Madison Square Garden

Penn Station

7th Avenue Fashion Avenue

Fashion Institue of Technology